GS 1361

marriage in church after divorce

A discussion document from a Working Party commissioned by the House of Bishops of the Church of England

CHURCH HOUSE
PUBLISHING

Church House Publishing
Church House
Great Smith Street
London SW1P 3NZ

ISBN 0 7151 3833 2

Published in 2000 for the House of Bishops of the General Synod of the
Church of England by Church House Publishing
Third impression 2000

*This report has only the authority of the House of Bishops' Working Party that
produced it.*

Acknowledgement
Extracts from The Revised Standard Version of the Bible (RSV) are copyright
1946, 1952, © 1971, 1973 by the Division of Christian Education of the
National Council of Churches of Christ in the USA.

Printed in England by Halstan & Co. Ltd
Designed by Jordan Design

contents

Preface: Note by the House of Bishops   v
Foreword by the chairman of the Working Party   ix
Summary of the Working Party's approach   xi
Glossary   xiii

1. **Introduction**   1
2. **Theological and liturgical questions**   10
3. **The social context**   20
4. **The legal context in Church and State**   23
5. **The wider Church context**   30
6. **Towards a common policy**   37
7. **Services of prayer and dedication**   41
8. **Conclusion and consequential recommendations**   45
9. **Summary of recommendations**   50

Appendix 1: Draft code of practice   52
Appendix 2: The 1957 Act of the Canterbury Convocation   62
Appendix 3: Extract from *Marriage and the Church's Task*   65
Appendix 4: Marriage statistics 1976–96   87
Appendix 5: Draft Guidelines put forward by the House of Bishops in 1985   88

Notes   93
Membership of the Working Party   96
List of those who submitted evidence   97
Further reading   98

preface:
note by the House of Bishops

1 The attached report is from a Working Party, under the chairmanship of the Bishop of Winchester, which was commissioned by the House specifically in response to a Motion carried by the General Synod in November 1994. It is nevertheless an issue – as explained in Chapter 1 of the report – which the Church has been actively engaged in, one way or another, since the 1970s. Given that further marriage after divorce is part of a much wider picture relating to marriage generally, the House decided to initiate more theological work on marriage prior to the issuing of this report (and other Church initiatives concerning marriage – such as the review of marriage law in relation to banns, etc., and the appointment of a Marriage and Family Policy Officer). In our Statement on Marriage, issued on 20 September 1999[1], we set out the heart of what the church believes and teaches about marriage. The Statement therefore sets the context for this report, and provides a basis for a programme of teaching on these matters.

2 The Church has a considerable pastoral ministry in helping people who are called to marriage to prepare for it and to enter into it. Such ministry continues in the support and care of people in their married and family life. That care and nurture includes those for whom marriage involves struggle which sometimes ends in marriage breakdown. The Church is often a community of support and help for couples who have been through the trauma of divorce. Those who return to marriage after divorce sometimes request the ministry of the Church. As part of our pastoral ministry to people seeking marriage, the Church needs to

respond to these approaches. This report is designed to help the Church make that response with a greater degree of consistency and confidence.

3   In our Statement, we said this on further marriage:

> ... should the Church as a whole decide upon an alternative [practice], it will be on precisely the same principles that have guided it up to this point: that marriage is an unconditional commitment for life; that a further marriage is an exceptional act; that it must be approached with great honesty and circumspection; and that the Church itself, through its ministry, has a part to play in deciding whether or not a marriage in such circumstances should take place in the context of church worship.

These are the guiding principles that undergird the House's approach to this issue, and we commend the reading of our Statement in full as background to this report, which itself begins with an affirmation that "marriage is a gift of God in creation and a means of grace and ...should always be undertaken as a lifelong commitment".

4   The House is clear that there should be no change in the Church's position on this matter without a clear mandate from the Church, and we issue this report now for consultation in dioceses so that we can gather views on its recommendations before deciding in what terms ourselves to report to the General Synod. The Working Party did of course frame its recommendations in the light of existing guidelines operating in

dioceses, but the House considers it important that dioceses and parishes should have an opportunity to consider the report in view of its implications for local pastoral practice.

5 Between now and the end of March next year, Diocesan Synods are asked to respond specifically to the following propositions:
1) Do you accept the principle that there are circumstances in which a divorced person may be married in church during the lifetime of a former spouse?
2) a. Do you support the recommendations of the Working Party summarized in Chapter 9 of the report as being the right way to proceed?
   b. If not, what do you consider to be the shortcomings of the recommendations?

We envisage that, after taking soundings from deaneries and parishes as they see fit, Diocesan Synods would vote on motions inviting them to express support or otherwise for the above questions.

6 We ask that details of any relevant motions and amendments debated by each Synod (with voting figures), together with any supplementary commentary a diocese may wish to offer, be sent to the Secretary of the House, Jonathan Neil-Smith, **by no later than 30 March 2001**. The responses from Diocesan Synods will be collected so that they will be considered by the House with a view to it reporting on these matters to the General Synod before the end of 2001.

7 The House is grateful to the Bishop of Winchester and the members of his working party for their report. We commend it now to dioceses so that the clergy and people can prayerfully consider its recommendations.

Church House,
London SW1P 3NZ
January 2000

(on behalf of the House)

✠ **GEORGE CANTUAR**
Chairman of the House of Bishops

foreword by the chairman of the Working Party

It is 17 years since the General Synod resolved, by large majorities in all three Houses, that there are circumstances in which a divorced person may be married in church during the lifetime of a former partner. The Working Party has seen its task as primarily to follow through the logic of that Synodical Resolution in the light of current pastoral practice in dioceses. We recognize the sincerely held views of those who take an indissolubilist line, but propose nothing that alters the Church's traditional teaching that marriage should always be undertaken as a lifelong commitment, nor do we propose any alteration to the existing statutory protection of clerical consciences on this matter.

Many in the Church have felt a need for greater coherence and consistency of practice in the whole area of further marriage; and many who look to the Church of England for its ministry find our present positions contradictory in principle, and simply unfair, because uneven and unpredictable, in their experience. We therefore offer recommended criteria and procedures, developed from what we consider best current diocesan practice, which we hope will gain the maximum degree of acceptance across dioceses. In doing so, we are not proposing, nor would wish to propose, indiscriminate further marriage. We do nevertheless recommend, unanimously, a straightforward procedure whereby clergy may, by way of exception, solemnize further marriages of divorced persons, with a former partner still living, where circumstances meet the appropriate pastoral criteria, in such a way that this is no longer inconsistent with the declared mind of the Church.

On behalf of the Working Party, I want to thank all those who have assisted us in our task, particularly the representatives of other Churches; John Haskey of the Office of National Statistics; Brian Hanson, the General Synod's Legal Adviser; and very particularly our staff, Nigel Barnett, Jonathan Neil-Smith and Jane Melrose, who served the work excellently and with marvellous patience and humour. I thank warmly, too, the members of the Working Party themselves.

We commend this report for consideration by the House of Bishops.

✠ **MICHAEL WINTON**

September 1998

[Factual information in the report was updated in September 1999.]

summary of the Working Party's approach

1. We hold steadfastly to the view that marriage is a gift of God in creation and a means of grace and that it should always be undertaken as a lifelong commitment. Nothing in this report should therefore be taken to imply any change in the Church of England's teaching on marriage. We nevertheless believe that it can be said of two living people that they were married and are no longer married. We therefore concur with the General Synod's view (as expressed in 1981) that there are circumstances in which a divorced person may be married in church during the lifetime of a former spouse.

2. We do not, however, envisage indiscriminate opportunity for further marriage in church. Nor do we recommend a panel-based mechanism for handling applications for such marriages. We do, nevertheless, believe that it is desirable to achieve the maximum degree of consistency in the Church's practice, and recommend a common set of pastoral criteria, principles and procedures to this end. Further marriages should normally only proceed if the incumbent – whose decision it would remain – is satisfied (after reference to the diocesan bishop) that the couple has sufficiently met those pastoral criteria.

3. We reaffirm the conscientious right of clergy not to solemnize such marriages.

4 In recommending criteria and procedures for further marriage after divorce, we are also clear that this may not always be appropriate and we therefore recommend that the alternative option of a service of prayer and dedication should continue to be available.

glossary

In the report:

1. **Incumbent** includes:
   (a) the incumbent of a benefice;
   (b) a priest licensed as priest-in-charge of a parish in respect of which rights of presentation are suspended;
   (c) a vicar in a team ministry to the extent that the duties of an incumbent are assigned to him/her by a scheme under the Pastoral Measure 1983 or his/her licence from the bishop; and
   (d) the minister in charge of any church or place of worship situated in an extraparochial place which is licensed for marriages.

2. **Bishop** means the bishop of the diocese concerned.

3. **Further marriage** means the marriage in church of persons one or both of whom have been divorced with a former spouse still living.

4. **Parish church** means a parish church as defined by s.6 of the Marriage Act 1949, a parish centre of worship as defined by s.29 of the Pastoral Measure, or a chapel licensed for marriages by the bishop under ss.20 and 21 of the Marriage Act 1949.

1: introduction

1.1 This report arose from a Private Member's Motion in the November 1994 Group of Sessions of the General Synod from the Revd Paul Needle. It was carried in the following amended form:

> That this Synod request the House of Bishops to consider the present practice of marriage in Church after divorce and to report.

In March 1995 the House of Bishops' Standing Committee agreed to set up a Working Party with the following remit:

(i) to review the present practice;

(ii) to consider possibilities for change;

(iii) to prepare a report for the House of Bishops.

1.2 In approaching our task we have been acutely conscious that this is an area where the Church of England has in the past found it very difficult to reach a common mind. Although the Church has wrestled with this issue and tried to identify circumstances and processes in which such marriages could take place, it has not so far been able to find a sufficient degree of consensus behind any particular way forward. This report thus follows in the wake of a number of other Church of England reports on marriage and divorce in recent years:

- *Putting Asunder*, 1966 – Report of the Archbishop of Canterbury's Commission on Divorce Law Reform (chaired by the Right Revd Robert Mortimer, Bishop of Exeter);
- *Marriage, Divorce and the Church*, 1971 – Report of the Archbishop of Canterbury's Commission on the Christian Doctrine of Marriage (The Root Report);

- *Marriage and the Church's Task*, 1978 – Report of the General Synod Marriage Commission (The Lichfield Report);
- *Marriage and the Standing Committee's Task*, 1983 – a response by the Standing Committee of the General Synod to a General Synod Motion; and
- *The Draft Marriage Regulation* (GS 669) – The Report of the House of Bishops, 1985.

We acknowledge the great debt we owe to the very thorough work undertaken by those who produced this series of reports. We see no need to go over all the well-trodden ground again. However, it may be helpful to trace the following brief history of these reports.

Putting Asunder

1.3 The Mortimer Commission confined itself expressly to civil divorce law and did not consider the matrimonial doctrine and discipline of the Church of England. It nevertheless recommended a radical reform of the basis for civil divorce by proposing that the matrimonial offence as the ground of action for divorce – with its distinction between the 'innocent' and the 'guilty' party – be abolished and be replaced with the recognition of the irretrievable breakdown of marriage: a proposal that was reflected in the Divorce Reform Act of 1969.

The Root Report

1.4 Although the Root Commission came to the view in its survey of biblical sources that Jesus had taught that 'in the purposes of God marriage was meant to be permanent' (p.94), and

2

recognized that Jesus' teachings about marriage were very demanding, it nevertheless concluded that the Church was free to draw up its own rules where a couple fell short of the demands of Jesus' teaching and a marriage died. The Commission judged that there was a growing consensus among Christian people to the effect that some marriages, however well-intentioned when undertaken, did break down; that divorced partners could enter into new unions that bore the hallmarks of a satisfactory marriage; and that Christian congregations were not scandalized by the presence of such couples in their midst. It went on to set out the conditions in which it would be appropriate to allow second or subsequent marriages in church, recommending – without setting out specific procedures – that discreet enquiries be made regarding the discharge of obligations arising from the previous marriage, into the attitudes of the persons wishing to remarry, and as to their intention that the union be permanent. While discretion would ultimately remain with the incumbent, the report seemed to envisage that the bishop or his advisers would undertake the necessary enquiries.

1.5 In a series of debates in the General Synod in 1972/4, the report did not have a smooth passage. Some rejected the possibility of further marriage after divorce on theological grounds; others argued strongly that permitting people to take lifelong vows twice would weaken the Church's witness to the Christian ideal; there was also a dislike of arguing on the basis of a perceived consensus, rather than on the rightness of the case; and anxiety about the exposed position of the parish priest. The debate on the report was also taking place in the context of spiralling divorce rates in the wake of the Divorce Reform Act 1969. A new range of issues surfaced with concern that the State's understanding of marriage was diverging from that held by the Church. In 1974, the General Synod came to the view that further consideration of proposals for the further marriage of divorced persons in church should be deferred until there had been a fresh examination of the Christian doctrine of marriage and of marriage discipline in the Church of England.

The Lichfield Report

1.6 This Commission followed up the General Synod's 1974 Resolution and analysed the theological position in some depth. It was, however, unable to reach a common mind on the question of further marriage in church after divorce, but recommended by a majority that the Church of England should take steps to revise its regulations to permit a divorced person, with the bishop's permission, to be married in church during the lifetime of a former spouse, using one of the existing permitted rites (with the addition of an appropriate invariable Preface). The new procedure was to be reviewed after a specified period of years. The report was referred to diocesan synods in 1979/80: 18 dioceses voted in favour of further marriage in church in certain circumstances; 17 voted against; and 3 felt that no change should be made in the Church's marriage discipline.

Marriage and the Standing Committee's Task ['Option G']

1.7 In July 1981, the General Synod carried the following amended Private Member's Motion by large majorities in all three Houses:

> *That this Synod*
>
> (a) *believes that marriage should always be undertaken as a lifelong commitment;*
>
> (b) *considers that there are circumstances in which a divorced person may be married in church during the lifetime of a former partner; and*
>
> (c) *asks the Standing Committee to prepare a report setting out a range of procedures for cases where it is appropriate for a divorced person to marry in church in a former partner's lifetime, for consideration by the Synod before any action is taken to repeal or modify the relevant existing regulations and resolutions of the Convocations.*

1.8 In response to this motion, the Standing Committee produced its report, *Marriage and the Standing Committee's Task*, in April 1983. This report built upon the earlier work of the Root and Lichfield Commissions and confined itself largely to setting out a range of possible procedures whereby divorced persons could, in the lifetime of a previous spouse, remarry in church. Arising from this the Synod asked the Standing Committee to bring forward draft regulations necessary to implement one of these, 'Option G', under which an incumbent would submit a form setting out the couple's circumstances to his bishop, who would in turn consult an advisory panel and then decide whether or not to give his permission.

1.9 The 'Option G proposals' also had a rough passage in the General Synod, as they were widely seen as overly bureaucratic, and pastorally insensitive. The Synod referred the draft regulations to the House of Bishops, and after bishops had undertaken consultations in their dioceses, the House reported to the Synod in February 1984 that those consultations indicated that the procedures in 'Option G' were not seen as the way forward and that the House had therefore decided, unanimously, not to return the draft 'Option G' regulations back to Synod for final approval.

House of Bishops' Proposals (1984/5)

1.10 In rejecting 'Option G', the House of Bishops put forward an alternative procedure of its own, which was designed to be less complicated and more closely pastoral and personal in its approach. Draft Regulations to this effect – including provision for a service of prayer and dedication after a civil ceremony as a possible alternative – were provisionally approved by the General Synod in July 1984, and then referred to dioceses. In the event, only 12 Diocesan Synods approved the draft Regulation and 31 rejected it. The House of Bishops accordingly decided not to refer the draft Marriage Regulation to the General Synod for final approval.

1.11 The House of Bishops then issued a report (GS 669) affirming that the Marriage Resolutions of the Convocations of Canterbury and York (made in 1938, and strengthened by the former in an Act of Convocation in 1957) [see Appendix 2], prohibiting the use of the marriage service in the case of anyone with a former spouse still living, remained in force. The House nevertheless agreed:

(i) *that there are a substantial number in the Church who believe in good conscience that a 'second' marriage is possible in some cases;*

(ii) *that those clergy who take this considered view are free under the provision of civil law to allow such 'second' marriages and that a number are already doing so; and that*

(iii) *the ultimate decision in such cases must be a matter for the clergyman concerned. However the House hopes that clergy who wish to allow a 'second' marriage would seek the advice of their Bishops. The overall desire is to achieve as much pastoral consistency and fairness as possible in the current circumstances.*

1.12 The House's report also proposed that the provision in the Act of Convocation passed by the Upper and Lower Houses of the Canterbury Convocation in 1957[1] that '… no public service be held for those who have contracted a civil marriage after divorce…' be repealed, which the General Synod duly did in July 1985. The House approved and commended for use a service of prayer and dedication after a civil marriage in June 1985 (its use being permissible under either Canon B 4 or B 5).

Recent developments

1.13 Although there have been no major developments concerning the further marriage of divorced persons in church until the passage

7

of Mr Needle's Private Members' Motion in November 1994 (see para. 1.1 above), the following marriage-related matters have come before the Synod:

- *An Honourable Estate* (the report of a Working Party of the Synod's Standing Committee) was published in 1988. Although the report had its origin in a Synod Motion of the Bishop of Chichester passed in February 1984 in the context of a debate about the further marriage of divorced persons, its main focus was on the Church's legal obligation to marry all parishioners who were not divorced. The report considered a number of options, including universal civil marriage, but concluded with a strong reaffirmation of the Church of England's present role, and urged that full use should be made of the pastoral opportunities that it offered.

- In 1990, the Clergy (Ordination) Measure was passed by both the General Synod and Parliament. This put in place a procedure under Canon C 4 whereby prospective ordinands who had remarried in the lifetime of a former spouse, or whose spouse had done so, could, on application from the diocesan bishop, proceed to ordination provided the archbishop of the relevant province agreed to grant a faculty removing the impediment that would otherwise exist on those grounds.

- In 1995, *Something to Celebrate* (the report of a Working Party of the Board for Social Responsibility) was published. This was a major report on families and society. Drawing upon its survey of changing social patterns and Christian teaching, it sought to help families as they faced up to new challenges. Among its recommendations, it emphasized the importance of marriage preparation, and affirmed the work of the Family Life and Marriage Education (FLAME) network, which had developed in 1989 from the earlier work of the House of Bishops' Marriage Education Panel. In commending the report for further study and debate in the Church in November 1995, the General Synod strongly reaffirmed its belief that marriage provided the proper context for sexual relationships and the bringing up of children.

- In November 1996, the General Synod passed a Private Member's Motion from the Revd Richard Hanford calling for a review of the current procedures for banns of marriage. The setting up of this review has been delayed pending the availability of resources, but in April 1999 the Archbishops' Council agreed to set up a Review Group which would look not only at banns, but also the possibility of universal civil preliminaries, authorized marriage venues (including residence qualifications), the permitted times for marriages, ecumenical issues relating to the solemnization of marriage, and other aspects of marriage law. This review, which is not expected to report until the latter half of 2000, coincides with a Government review of the civil registration system. The hope is that recommendations from the Church's Review Group relating to the provisions of the Marriage Act 1949 could be tied in with the Government's own legislative intentions.

2: theological and liturgical questions

2.1 While we regard the close study of the relevant biblical passages in the New Testament as an essential starting point for any consideration of this subject, in approaching our task we recognized that a very comprehensive analysis of the biblical and theological background is contained in the earlier reports referred to in paragraph 1.2 above. In particular we commend to readers *Marriage and the Church's Task*, which includes a detailed exposition of the various biblical texts on marriage[1] (see Appendix 3). We summarize the results of the prolonged and varied debate which has taken place in the course of this century about these texts and their exposition in the following observations, which are, of course, too brief to do full justice to it:

(a) Jesus understood the Mosaic provisions for divorce as a legal concession to moral weakness, and taught that any departure from the norm of lifelong fidelity was a failure to live up to the purpose of God in creation.

(b) He did not, however, mean by this to declare the Mosaic provisions illegitimate in legal terms, or pretend to abrogate them.

(c) While Jesus himself, in all probability, did not elaborate his judgement against divorce in any way, the apostles, in interpreting its bearing upon specific practical questions, understood it to allow certain qualifications. So in St Matthew (19.9) we find the exceptive clause concerning *porneia* ('unchastity') and in St Paul (1 Corinthians 7) the provision that the believer deserted by an unbelieving partner 'is not bound'.

(d) The patristic Church, however, understood these qualifications *not* to amount to an approval of actual remarriage, only of separation. They increasingly understood Jesus' words describing divorce and remarriage as 'adultery' to have not just a moral but an ontological force – i.e. that the marriage still subsisted after divorce.

(e) The Western Catholic tradition, understanding the words from Ephesians 5, that marriage was a 'great mystery', to mean that it was a sacrament, began to interpret Christian marriage within the context of its understanding of the Christian sacraments and to attribute to it a persisting 'character' comparable to that conferred by baptism. By the late Middle Ages, therefore, the doctrine of Christian marriage had reached a decisive form.

(f) This doctrine was rejected by the Continental Reformers in the course of their revision of the medieval doctrine of the sacraments. They believed that the qualifying clauses in Matthew and Paul allowed for both divorce and remarriage of an innocent party in response to a very limited range of grave marital offences. From Romans 7 they derived the notion of the 'moral death' of the offender, which entitled the innocent party to be treated as a widow or widower. At one point in the sixteenth century, the English Church seemed likely to follow this lead, but in the event never did.

2.2 Our own approach starts from the conviction (corresponding to the principle expressed in Canon B 30) that marriage is intended by God to be a permanent and lifelong union, and must always be undertaken as such. As is stated in *The Book of Common Prayer*, Holy Matrimony *'is an honourable estate, instituted of God in the time of man's innocency, signifying unto us the mystical union that is betwixt Christ and his Church'*. This implies that marriage is more than a contract of cohabitation between two individuals: it is a state of life given to men and women as a gift in Creation, to reflect the faithfulness of God's own relation to humankind as we see it in Christ. As it has been expressed by the Anglican-Roman Catholic International Commission:

> *Covenanted human love points beyond itself to the covenantal love and fidelity of God and God's will that marriage should be a means of universal blessing and love ... Since it also points to the saving love of God, embodied in Christ's love for the Church (Ephesians 5.25), it is open to a still deeper sacramentality within the life and communion of Christ's own body.*[2]

It has, therefore, its own proper structure, through which couples are led to imitate for one another God's love for them, and that structure includes permanence as one of its chief elements.

2.3 But we do not hold the view that when a marriage has completely failed, it continues to subsist in a shadowy fashion: we believe that it can be said in a literal sense of two living people that they *were* married and are *no longer* married. (It should be added in parenthesis, perhaps, that it needs pastoral discernment to determine whether a relationship still exists or not in a particular case. In an age of comparatively straightforward divorce proceedings which may still favour speedy divorce, a decree from a court may not be the last word on the matter. We should not overlook the incidence of cases in which couples who divorce think better of it, and marry each other a second time.)

2.4 We take it as implied by Jesus' teaching that where a marriage has broken down, there is responsibility and fault to be acknowledged before God. It is not, however, for those not immediately involved to point the finger and say just where the fault lies; it is for the former partners themselves to seek an honest view of their failure, a process in which the Church may assist in a pastorally supportive role. Where there is honesty and openness to the searching work of the Holy Spirit in the conscience, the Church's duty and privilege is to assure the believer of forgiveness and acceptance in Christ. This *may* take the form of supporting him or her in a new marriage. But it would be unwise to suggest that this is the only, or even the normal way in which the word of forgiveness is offered. When 'forgiveness' comes to be used as a code-word for permission to remarry, forgiveness itself is not being appreciated or understood, and the gospel of freedom from sin is being mistaken for a means of self-justification. Nor is it necessarily the appropriate thing for every person who has been married and is no longer married to undertake a new marriage. Our presumption in what follows is simply that it may *sometimes* be so, and that this needs discernment in each particular case.

2.5 We should add that although our own view is not 'indissolubilist' as that term is usually used – that is, we do not believe that every Christian marriage persists in being until the death of one partner, irrespective of separation or divorce – we are aware that a significant number within the Church of England hold that view, and that it can claim with some justice to represent the traditional position of the Church of England. No proposal for change would be acceptable to the Church of England if it simply rode roughshod over the conviction of some members, including some priests, that a divorced couple is still, in a real if indeterminate sense, married.

Dispensation from vows

2.6 We believe that it would be inappropriate for the Church to have any role in formalizing or finalizing a divorce. We do not support the proposal that the Church of England should provide a liturgical form of release from marriage vows. The desire to ensure a pastoral role for the Church at this point runs the risk of turning it into an agent of divorce. The vows are not something separate from the marriage itself; they are the spoken expression of the marriage covenant and live or die with that covenant. If it can be seen that the covenant has no surviving reality, then it can be seen that the vows have none; while there is a serious question in somebody's mind whether he or she is still bound by past marriage vows, then there is a serious question whether he or she is bound by the past marriage, and the Church is not to dismiss such a question lightly by offering some ceremony that will put it to rest.

2.7 The analogy sometimes suggested between such a procedure and release from religious vows is not, to our mind, a persuasive one. The Church stands in a different relation to vows of religious communities and those taken in marriage. In the latter, the couple vow to each other before God with the Church as a witness. As the Bishop of Portsmouth put it in evidence to the Working Party, '*... we do not have a liturgical tradition which could be said to put the priest in the position of "receiving" the vows in such a way that he could "release" them'*. True, we can say that the Church's presence at a marriage, witnessing it and declaring God's blessing, *elevates* it, as Jesus 'adorned and beautified with his presence and first miracle that he wrought' the marriage at Cana in Galilee. In this context the language of 'sacramental significance' has had an established place in Anglican thought about marriage, which *'signifies unto us the mystical union which is betwixt Christ and his church'*. Yet this does not make the Church a *primary actor* in the exchange of vows, let alone a primary actor in the abrogation of them.

2.8 If any releasing of vows is to take place, our view is that this can only be done by the couple themselves. If recent secular legislation succeeds in its stated objective of reducing acrimony in divorce proceedings, this should increase the scope for some form of 'mutual release' from the marriage vows, alongside whatever mutual arrangements are made in respect of property and pension rights, and access to children. There could be considerable benefits for people not only being legally 'free' after a divorce but also in knowing that their former spouse had accepted that fact by way of a release from the marriage vows. We can envisage circumstances in which couples may find it beneficial to do this in the context of a mediation process. While for the reasons given above we do not consider it appropriate for the Church of England to provide a liturgy for the release from vows, it is important that parish priests should be known to be available in a pastoral capacity at the time of marriage breakdown, divorce, and preparation for further marriage.

The place of a penitential element in the marriage service

2.9 We have considered whether the incorporation of a penitential element into the marriage service would be appropriate in cases of further marriage. There appears to be considerable variation of practice elsewhere in the Anglican Communion on this matter. In some provinces the liturgy remains unaltered, whereas in others a specific 'introduction for the remarriage of divorced persons'[3] concludes with the bride and bridegroom making a general confession, followed in the usual way by the priest pronouncing absolution. The introduction to one such service describes Christian marriage as *'both a civil contract and a spiritual union into which the couple enter by the exchange of solemn vows made before God'*. It speaks of the seriousness of breaking a civil contract and the even greater seriousness of breaking lifelong vows before God. The priest then goes on to say that members of the congregation 'may wonder how it is that this [further] marriage can have the Church's blessing'. This statement follows:

> *The bishop himself is satisfied that in this instance there is no prospect of re-establishing a true marriage relationship between the partners of the former marriage(s). N. and N. have been interviewed and the bishop is assured that there is due penitence for the failure of the previous marriage(s) and a knowledge of God's forgiveness as well as a readiness to forgive.*[4]

2.10 Judging by the example quoted above, formal liturgical provision of this kind can make the Church sound publicly defensive and can seem inappropriate as an introduction to an act of worship. It is also peculiarly difficult to write an introduction which does justice to the very different marital histories of the couples concerned. A deserted partner divorced against his or her will coming for further marriage some 20 years later may be exceptional, but the lack of flexibility in a standard preface could be pastorally damaging in such a case. If our approach is to be a pastoral rather than a legal one, then the liturgy should reflect such priorities.

2.11 We do take the view, however, that some divorced people need to have the burdens of the breakdown of the previous relationship lifted from them. It may be that a service of penitence could form part of the marriage preparation rather than expect the marriage liturgy itself to incorporate this element as well as celebrating the new relationship. We sought the views of the Liturgical Commission who advised against a different form of service for the marriage itself where one of the parties was divorced, judging that the moral and pastoral concerns are best met at the time of the marriage ceremony by this being as joyful, celebratory and forward-looking as any *other* marriage. The Commission also believed that *everyone* present at a marriage, and not simply the couple, needed to approach God in penitence, and they favoured the optional use of the Collect for Purity for this purpose. As we understand it, this is not a penitential prayer, but it may prove an appropriate option in some marriage services. We agreed with the Commission's view that the central core of the service should be the same in such circumstances, and that any attempt to differentiate the marriage of previously divorced people should be avoided. Nevertheless, we judged that the service should not deny the reality of the situation, but believe that, particularly given the wide range of prayers available in the *Common Worship* material, it is best to leave such matters and how they are reflected in the service to the discretion of the officiating minister.

Church nullity procedures

2.12 We noted the nullity procedures of the Roman Catholic Church (see para. 5.1 below) and the earlier consideration of the feasibility of adopting a process of this kind as set out in *Marriage and the Standing Committee's Task.*[5] We were not persuaded that this process would be an appropriate way forward for the Church of England and concur in this respect with the view of the Lichfield Report *(Marriage and the Church's Task)* that:

> ... it would be regarded as an artificial way of dealing with the problems of marriage breakdown, and one bristling with practical difficulties of organisation and procedure. It would introduce a quasi-judicial process into an area of church life where, at present, none exists ... we should prefer to see a pastoral rather than a legal procedure.[6]

3: the social context

3.1 There have been very significant changes in marriage and society in recent years as these statistics for England and Wales testify:

- Over a quarter of all couples who married in the late 1970s and early 1980s had divorced by the end of 1994.[1]
- Whereas 23% of couples who married in 1961 had divorced during the first 30 years of their marriage, this same proportion was reached during the first 10 years of marriage among those who married in 1981. If divorce rates were to remain unchanged at recent levels, 41% (i.e. about two in every five) of new marriages would ultimately end in divorce.[2]
- Although marriage is still popular, in that just under seven in every ten of the population might expect to be married by the age of 50, the divorce rate in England and Wales of 14 per thousand married couples per year is one of the highest in the European Union.[3]
- In addition, the proportions divorced within the early years of marriage have increased more rapidly for groups of couples married in successive years than have the proportions divorced after longer periods of marriage. For example, the proportions of couples married in 1961 who had divorced within 5 and 15 years of their marriage were 2% and 13%, whereas the proportions for those marrying in 1976 were 10% and 27% respectively.[4]
- An increasing number of children have been affected by divorce; if divorce rates were to persist unchanged at recent levels, 28% – more than one in four – of children living in married couple families would experience divorce in their family before reaching the age of 16.[5]

- A growing proportion of marriages are further marriages after divorce: in 1971, 16% of all marriages involved one or both parties remarrying after divorce; by 1996 this proportion had grown to 40%.[6]
- Other factors being constant, the younger the age at marriage, the larger the risk of divorce – and this effect applies no matter how long the marriage has lasted. The proportion of teenage spouses whose marriage has ended in divorce has always been high – approximately double that for spouses who married for the first time between the ages of 20 and 24.[7]
- Couples are marrying for the first time later in life, typically at 26 for women and 28 for men.[8]
- The incidence of premarital co-habitation has been growing steadily: of those women marrying for the first time in the mid-1960s only about 5% had lived with their future husband before their marriage, but this proportion had reached about 70% of women marrying for the first time in the early 1990s.[9]

3.2 The implications of these changes in marriage for the family and society have recently been analysed in *Something to Celebrate*, the report (1995) of a Working Party set up by the Church of England's Board for Social Responsibility. We see no need to duplicate that work, but rather view our task as assisting the Church to address the reality whereby two in every five marriages involve at least one divorced partner. Indeed, despite the official position of the Church as set out in Chapter 1 above, in 1996 7,270 weddings involving a divorced person were in fact solemnized by clergy of the Church of England and the Church in Wales (see Appendix 4), 10% of all Anglican marriages in these two Churches. Although this is a small proportion of all Church weddings, it is nevertheless clear evidence that, despite the inability of the Church to agree changes in practice, marriage in church after divorce is becoming an increasingly common occurrence in the Church of England, with some clergy being content to conduct such weddings. It also contrasts sharply with the corresponding proportions – in 1996 – of 62% for the Methodist Church (see para. 5.2 below) and 64% for the United Reformed Church (see para. 5.4 below), although it should be noted that these figures include members of other denominations turning to those churches for a 'church wedding'.

4: the legal context in Church and State

4.1 Canon A 5 stipulates that the doctrine of the Church of England is grounded in the Holy Scriptures and in such teachings of the ancient Fathers and Councils of the Church as are agreeable to the said Scriptures. In particular such doctrine is to be found in *The Thirty-Nine Articles of Religion*, *The Book of Common Prayer* and the *Ordinal*. Thus according to *The Book of Common Prayer*, Holy Matrimony *'is an honourable estate, instituted of God in the time of man's innocency, signifying unto us the mystical union that is betwixt Christ and his Church'*.

4.2 Both the law of the State and canon law accept that marriage is a contract but not merely a contract: out of the marriage contract something greater than a contract develops, i.e. the union of one man with one woman for life. The contract is one which must have been freely entered upon by both parties to the marriage, and they must both have been free to make the contract, neither being already the spouse of another, nor suffering from any disqualification, and it must have been their common intention that the union should last until one of them should die, and should be a union to the exclusion of all others.

4.3 Since the introduction of divorce into matrimonial law, however, the State must now be taken to say that, following the marriage, there is a new *legal status*; while the Church maintains that what results is something more – a *relationship* akin in certain respects to the relationship existing between parent and child or of brother and sister. In the words of F. J. Sheed, *'relationship differs from status in this: that it is a God-made thing, which man cannot alter. God alone can bring it into being. But status depends upon the will of the State, and status can be varied by the State.'*[1]

4.4 Since the structure of marriage itself is a gift of the Creator, neither the Church nor the State has an unrestricted authority to legislate about it. It is, of course, perfectly within the Church's competence to make legislative provisions with regard to incidentals – the form, the time, and place of the ceremony, for example. Nor does the Church deny the right of the State to terminate the consequences of the legal status. As the State has the right to remove a child from the control of a parent who has abused that control, so by a decree of divorce it may grant freedom from legal ties which bind a husband and wife together. But this does not imply the power, in Church or State, to *'put asunder those whom God has joined together'*. The terms of the marriage covenant are created neither by Church nor State, but are, in legal terminology, 'of divine law', which is why the Church in the West has never ventured to grant divorces, but has at most confined itself to permitting another marriage in some cases where it is clear that the former marriage no longer exists.

4.5 This was the background to a disagreement in 1984 among lawyers who advised the House of Bishops about the draft Regulation which would have given effect to the proposed arrangements for 'Option G'. The majority believed that the draft

Regulation was in conflict with Canon B 30, because a second marriage in the lifetime of a former partner would be inconsistent with the statement in the Canon that *'marriage is in its nature permanent and lifelong, for better for worse, till death do us part …'*. These lawyers suggested that a dispensing power for the bishop be added to the Canon. A minority of lawyers believed that the phrase *'in its nature'* did not exclude the recognition of the end of a marriage *de facto*.

4.6 Under the general law there is a legal obligation on a minister to marry those who are entitled by law to be married in the parish church. By the Matrimonial Causes Act, 1965, section 8, the cleric is relieved of this obligation in the case where there has been a divorce and the former partner of one of the parties is still living. The incumbent's obligation to officiate at weddings pre-dates any statute and is derived from pre-Reformation canon law. When Parliament first laid down formalities for the solemnization of marriage in Lord Hardwicke's Act of 1753, it required all marriages (other than those for Jews and Quakers) to be according to the rites and ceremonies of the Church of England. Divorce was available by Act of Parliament, and was extremely rare (typically with only one or two cases per year) but, until the Marriage Act of 1836, further marriage after divorce was only possible in church (except for Jews and Quakers) and it was the duty of clergy to conduct such services. Between 1753 and 1836, there was therefore a legal entitlement to be married in church after divorce, albeit an extremely rare occurrence.

4.7 The 1836 Act, however, introduced more or less the present range of options: regular Church of England marriages; marriage in a registered religious building for other denominations; and civil marriages. Further marriage after divorce was thus available through a civil ceremony. Some measure of protection for clerical consciences was included in the Matrimonial Causes Act of 1857 which relieved clergy of the obligation to marry the guilty party in adultery cases where the former partner was still living, although they did have to make the church available. The Matrimonial Causes Act of 1937 (the so-called Herbert Act) no longer obliged clergy to marry any divorced person, or to make their church available. The clergy 'conscience clause' remains unaffected by the Family Law Act 1996 and, as stated above, is now included in the Matrimonial Causes Act 1965. This Act also allows clergy to forbid the use of their parish church for further marriages involving a divorced person conducted by other clergy.

4.8 In 1983 *Marriage and the Standing Committee's Task* concluded (para. 16) that:

> ... *So far as the parishioner who has been divorced and whose former partner is still alive is concerned, it is a fact that he no longer has the legal right to be married in church. Accordingly, any question of marriage in church in such circumstances is wholly a matter for the Church which is clearly entitled to establish (without any conflict with the State) her own domestic tribunals or pastoral criteria for determining whether or not she will permit such a marriage to take place in church.*

4.9 The position regarding the Church's own stipulations concerning the further marriage of divorced persons in church is complex. The 1888 Lambeth Conference resolved that, based on Scripture, the Church could not recognize divorce on grounds other than those of fornication or adultery, and that even in these cases the guilty party should not have the further marriage blessed in church during the lifetime of the innocent party. In 1938 Resolutions against the further marriage of divorced persons were passed by the Convocations of Canterbury and York. The Upper House of Convocation of Canterbury followed this up by declaring an Act of Convocation in 1957 reaffirming the 1938 Regulations, the third of which unambiguously stated that:

> ... in order to maintain the principle of lifelong obligation which is inherent in every legally contracted marriage and is expressed in the plainest terms in the Marriage Service, the Church should not allow the use of that Service in the case of anyone who has a former partner still living.

4.10 This Act of Convocation remains the Church's formal position although, while it carries moral force, it is not legally binding on the clergy. Canon B 30 states that '... marriage is in its nature permanent and lifelong ...' and although divorce is not cited as an impediment to marriage in Canons B 31 and B 32, it may be implied when reading the three canons together.

4.11 In order to authorize by canon the further marriage of divorced people in church who have a previous spouse still living, one option would be to amend Canon B 30 (referred to in para. 4.5

27

above) along the lines of the following:

> *4. Recognizing that a marriage may break down irretrievably and be terminated by a decree of divorce made under civil law, in such a case the incumbent shall have discretion, to be exercised in accordance with a Code of Practice approved by the House of Bishops, to marry either party according to the rites and ceremonies of the Church of England during the lifetime of his or her former partner.*

In the event of this amendment to Canon B 30, the 1957 Act of Convocation of the Canterbury Convocation (see Appendix 2) would need to be revoked in its entirety.

4.12 If it be thought that no amendment to the canon should be made, an alternative way of proceeding would be to replace the 1957 Act of Convocation with a new Act of Synod. This Act could preface a form of words similar to that quoted in paragraph 4.11 above with the following:

> *That while affirming its adherence to our Lord's principle and standard of marriage as stated in Canon B 30, this Synod recognizes that the actual discipline of particular Christian Communions in this matter has varied widely from time to time and place to place, and holds that the Church of England is competent to enact such a discipline of its own in regard to marriage as may from time to time appear most salutary and efficacious. Now therefore this Act of Synod provides ... etc.*

Family Law Act 1996

4.13 In the light of concern at the increasing number of divorces, and the feeling that the divorce laws did little to help couples to stay together, the Family Law Act was passed in 1996. One of the aims of the 1996 law was to reduce acrimony in divorce proceedings. Under the previous legislation the most common grounds for divorce had been either 'unreasonable behaviour' (44 per cent of cases in 1995) or adultery (26 per cent of cases in 1995), as these had been ways of being granted a quick divorce. The other grounds were desertion (where the respondent had deserted the petitioner for at least two years), separation (where both parties had lived apart for two years and consented to a divorce), and establishing that the couple had lived apart for five years. Previously divorces on the grounds of adultery or unreasonable behaviour could be processed in as little as three months, thus encouraging petitions on these fault-based factors in order to speed up the proceedings. The new law builds in periods for reflection and consideration of at least nine months in the hope that the scope for saving the marriage can be explored. At the time of writing, it is not yet clear whether the relevant provisions of the Act (in Part II) will be implemented.

5: the wider Church context

The Roman Catholic Church

5.1 No one who has been validly married may remarry in the Roman Catholic Church while their former partner is alive, except for those who were partners in a failed marriage with a non-baptized person. In those cases, the local bishop or, more commonly, the Pope may grant a dissolution of the first bond to enable someone in this situation to marry a baptized person. The Roman Catholic Church also has a judicial process to determine the validity of marriages which it is asked to examine. This is applicable to all marriages (i.e. including those solemnized elsewhere). After due process and the conforming decision of two tribunals – one diocesan and one normally of the metropolitan – declaring the invalidity of a marriage, both parties would be free to marry in a Roman Catholic Church. In England, in order to avoid possible conflicts with the civil law, the usual practice is for the Marriage Tribunal to wait for the completion of civil divorce proceedings before initiating the nullity process. Marriage Tribunals are seen very much as a last resort, only to be approached once a marriage has definitely failed. While the pastoral care of the divorced and remarried (those who have not been granted either an annulment or dissolution) remains under review, there are no plans to review the legislation concerning marriage in church after divorce from a partner who is still living.

The Methodist Church

5.2 In 1946 the Methodist Conference accepted that a member of their Church who was the innocent party in a case of adultery could sue for divorce and that if such a person were granted a divorce, permission could be granted for them to remarry. Ministers were accordingly able to consider requests from such divorced persons to be remarried in Methodist churches, but ministers were not obliged to officiate at such marriages contrary to the dictates of their conscience. Although this procedure (SO 830) was originally designed for relatively rare cases, in 1996 there were 6,777 marriages in Methodist churches involving at least one divorced person, 62 per cent of all marriages in Methodist churches.

5.3 In 1998 the Methodist Conference adopted the report *Christian Preparation for Marriage*. It concluded with a statement of the Methodist Church's policy for all requests for marriage and directions for Good Practice in applying the Church's policy (both of which are printed in the official documents of the Church). Ministers are no longer obliged to determine what went wrong in a previous marriage, so as to try to discern who was the 'innocent' or 'guilty' party. Ministers who are prevented by conscience from ever officiating at the marriage service of a couple in particular circumstances (e.g. when one or both parties are divorced or the couple are co-habiting) should ensure that such couples are referred to a colleague not so prevented. After an initial interview with the minister, couples are encouraged to share in a process of marriage preparation, to which church members may contribute as well as the minister. At the end of a period of preparation a minister must reach with each couple a clear decision relating to their request for marriage: normally a minister will honour the couple's request, if made with understanding and faith, to participate in a marriage service in a Methodist church. In a case where a minister makes a pastoral judgement that a particular marriage in a particular church might have implications for the local congregation or community, the minister must consult the Chairman of the District and the Superintendent Minister before consent is given. Provision is also made for the circumstance where a minister personally has difficulties or uncertainties in acceding to a couple's request, to seek the help of a colleague in coming to a decision. If a request for a marriage in church is declined, it is deemed inappropriate for the minister to recommend a civil marriage in a Register Office followed immediately by a service of blessing in a church, on the grounds that whatever reasons ruled out the former would also apply theologically to the latter.

The United Reformed Church

5.4 While holding to the ideal of Christian marriage as a lifelong relationship, the United Reformed Church does allow further marriage after divorce in certain circumstances. Once satisfied that the previous marriage has been legally dissolved, the minister would discuss the circumstances surrounding the breakdown of the previous marriage and the satisfactory resolution of any resulting problems (such as the custody of children). In some cases the minister, in response to the couple's request and normally with the approval of the church, will conduct a separate service in which penitence can be expressed for the failure of the previous marriage, recognition be given that the relationship has ended, and in which the desire to seek a new beginning is made explicit. Liturgies for such services have been produced by individuals and are available. A further marriage of a divorcee can proceed when the minister and the church are satisfied that the circumstances are right. Such a service would differ little, if at all, from the normal marriage service. In 1996, 64 per cent of marriages in the United Reformed Church involved at least one divorced person.

The Church in Wales

5.5 The Church in Wales is in a very similar position to the Church of England in that, although it is disestablished, it operates under the same statute law, this being part of the vestiges of establishment that the Church has retained to the extent that it has not subsequently adopted different procedures. In 1938 the Bench of Bishops issued an instruction to all clergy effectively excommunicating any Church members who undertook further marriage during the lifetime of their former partner, and specifically forbidding clergy to exercise their discretion to marry such divorced persons in church or to allow their churches to be used for such marriages (though the former provision was abandoned as a general policy soon after the letter was published). A further letter from the bishops to the clergy in 1951 modified the 1938 stance somewhat by counselling and advising clergy not to solemnize such marriages. The matter has been under review since the setting up of a Working Party by the Bench of Bishops in 1971. Although this Working Party recommended no change in the Church's practice, the Governing Body refused to adopt the report in 1976, but a 1978 motion proposing provision for the remarriage of divorced persons during the lifetime of a former spouse was lost. The Governing Body nevertheless supported a service of blessing in such cases in 1979. A further review of the Church's discipline in this regard was initiated in 1994. A Bill which would have allowed further marriage was lost, narrowly, in the Governing Body in 1996, but the Bench of Bishops circulated a statement (with draft guidelines) to the Governing Body in April 1998 which allows further marriage at the discretion of individual clergy. Following comments made both by members of the Governing Body and clergy in diocesan meetings, the Bishops' Guidelines, proffering advice to clergy concerning the exercise of their legal right to solemnize further marriages, were issued in September 1998.

The Church of Scotland

5.6 The Church of Scotland has for many years had clearly defined procedures whereby ministers can lawfully solemnize the marriage of a divorced person who has a former partner still living. These place the onus on the minister to establish the circumstances of the couple, and the previous marriage, but do not oblige ministers to solemnize marriages against their conscience. Although the final decision rests with the local minister, provision is made within each Presbytery for him/her to consult with others should he/she feel the need to do so.

The Orthodox Churches[1]

5.7 The Orthodox Church regards the marriage bond as lifelong and indissoluble. But, recognizing that many marriages do in fact fail, as a concession to human frailty and sinfulness the Church under certain conditions allows divorce and further marriage in church, even when the other partner is still alive. Although a second or third marriage is permitted, the Church does not in any circumstances allow a fourth marriage (either after divorce or after the death of the previous partners).

5.8 In Britain the couple must first obtain a civil divorce, and they are then required to obtain a Church divorce from the local Church court (under the chairmanship of the diocesan bishop or his deputy). Further marriage in church is only possible if a Church divorce has first been obtained. In principle the ecclesiastical canons only allow divorce for certain specific reasons (chiefly adultery), but in practice it is granted on other grounds as well (e.g. irrevocable breakdown in personal relations). It is rare for the Church to withhold a divorce if the State has granted one. The church service books provide for further marriage after divorce, and this differs widely from that for a first marriage; several of the joyful ceremonies are omitted, and are replaced by penitential prayers. But today this service for a second marriage is not usually employed.

Other Churches

5.9 The Working Party also noted the practice in a number of Churches in Europe covered by the Porvoo and Meissen

Agreements. It nevertheless found that circumstances were often very different. In the Evangelical Church in Germany (EKD), for instance, all religious ceremonies must be preceded by a civil ceremony. There the EKD recognizes the validity of all civil marriages, and, as a general rule, would not refuse a religious ceremony to divorced persons who remarry (although a minister can opt out on grounds of conscience after consulting his Dean or Church Council). In Finland, such marriages can take place in church and the Evangelical Lutheran Church does not regard divorce as an impediment to such a marriage, although some pastors refuse on conscience grounds to remarry divorced persons.

6: towards a common policy

Diocesan practice

6.1 As already reported (para. 3.2 above), some 10 per cent of all Church of England marriages involve a divorced person with a spouse still living. We asked diocesan bishops to indicate their policies on the matter, and the majority of those who responded – over 30 (more than two-thirds of all diocesan bishops) – indicated that they did operate guidelines setting out the circumstances in which an incumbent could take such services, most of these being based on those put forward by the House of Bishops in 1985 (see Appendix 5). There were nevertheless considerable variations in practice both between and within dioceses.

6.2 Dioceses have chosen to interpret the bishops' guidelines in varying ways: in one or two dioceses the marriage of divorcees with a spouse still living is firmly discouraged, with the service of prayer and dedication after a civil ceremony being the norm; in others further marriage in church is not uncommon and the guidelines allow the incumbent, having observed some standard procedures, to judge whether it is pastorally the right course. There is little consistency as to whether the incumbent should consult the bishop (or his adviser), and the extent to which the PCC should be involved. We observed that in one diocese, Derby, a simplified version of the 'Option G' proposals was available on a permissory basis to those clergy seeking help with the discernment process; such cases were then referred to the bishop's adviser for guidance. Many dioceses, while recognizing that the last word rests with incumbents, nevertheless provide for them to be able to seek a second opinion. In the Diocese of

Liverpool, for example, the bishop works closely with an adviser who provides such help to incumbents. In all cases, the consciences of those clergy who do not wish to take such marriages are protected.

A national policy?

6.3 Having considered the variations in diocesan practice in the light of the available information, we consider that the present diversity of practice leads to inconsistency which may often be perceived as unfair. We recommend that national criteria and guidelines be drawn up, reflecting current best practice, with the aim that this will win broad acceptance across the Church of England. Although practices vary between dioceses, we noted that the position was just as likely to vary between parishes within the same diocese, depending on the view of the incumbent and/or PCC. We believe that there should be the maximum degree of consistency on this matter across the Church as a whole, and that the acceptance of a nationally agreed set of guidelines is central to achieving this.

The focus of decision-making

6.4 In considering where the focus of decision-making should lie, we accept that incumbents are the people in the best position to get to know the couple themselves and thus be able to form a pastoral judgement as to whether they should be married in church. We do, however, recognize that many incumbents still feel exposed under the current arrangements, and that some are undoubtedly reluctant to be drawn into the position of having to discriminate between requests from parishioners. Without proposing any transfer from incumbents of the decision whether or not to marry, we nevertheless judge that as a matter of good practice they should be required to seek outside advice. In doing so, we reject the introduction of a panel-based procedure which would be seen as inquisitorial and bureaucratic, and which we believe would not gain acceptance. Nor do we believe that it would be administratively workable, given the number of likely cases (an average of about three per week per diocese on current figures) and the attendant difficulty of operating such a system in today's more litigious climate. Rather, we recommend that incumbents refer all cases to their diocesan bishop with his role being to see that the right procedures have been followed, to offer whatever pastoral guidance he might feel appropriate, and to be available for consultation in difficult cases. It would be for individual bishops to decide how they would wish to handle this within their dioceses; some may wish such cases to be referred to a diocesan adviser appointed by them. The proposed procedure is set out in more detail in Appendix 1 (para. 4.7) but we would envisage a fairly straightforward process, neither administratively burdensome for the incumbent or bishop, nor too time-consuming for the couple, in which clear-cut cases would be handled swiftly. As well as engendering good practice, such referrals to the bishop would have the added advantage of minimizing inconsistencies of approach.

Collecting data

6.5 We recognize the difficulty of obtaining accurate information within dioceses about such further marriages. This is a serious disadvantage both for the purposes of assessing pastoral needs and in being able to present a comprehensive picture to the Lord Chancellor's Department and other such national bodies on matters relating to marriage and divorce and to make an effective response to press and other enquiries. A further benefit of the procedure recommended above would be that there would be a central point in each diocese where the statistics of such weddings could be kept.

A parish policy?

6.6 In some dioceses, clergy are encouraged to seek the views of their PCCs as to whether the parish church should be used for further marriages after divorce. We would wish to encourage the involvement of PCCs as far as the *general policy* is concerned (i.e. not discussing particular cases) as it is not only clerical consciences, but lay too, which are at issue in these cases. While accepting that incumbents have the final say about what services take place in churches in their care, we nevertheless recommend that they should seek to discuss their policy with their PCCs. It should, however, be noted (see para. 4.7 above) that incumbents cannot be obliged to make their parish church available for further marriages involving a divorced person as their position is protected by the provisions of the Matrimonial Causes Act 1965. This Act would need to be amended if it were felt desirable to enable PCCs to override incumbents on this matter. We do not recommend such a course.

7: services of prayer and dedication

7.1 When the Convocation Resolutions were passed in 1938, no provision was made for any public service in church following a civil marriage contracted by any person with a previous spouse still alive. Later, the Upper House of the Convocation of Canterbury expressly forbade such a public service, when the Resolutions became an Act of Convocation in 1957. However, that did not mean that those remarrying after divorce were denied access to the pastoral ministry of a priest. Some clergy would pray privately with the couple in church in addition to any wider pastoral support or counsel. Gradually this developed so that 'prayers at the chancel step' became a common description of what took place. There was a penitential character to the event expressed in the vesture of the priest (some bishops decreed that no stoles be worn), a limit on the number of people present, and a reluctance to pronounce any blessing on the couple. Hymns were often considered inappropriate since this would be to turn private prayers into a public service.

7.2 No authorized liturgy for the Church of England as a whole was published, although a number of diocesan bishops began to issue guidelines and even circulated what they considered to be appropriate forms of service, notwithstanding the Act of Convocation. By the 1970s, some clergy were conducting what they described as 'services of blessing'. These would be celebratory rather than penitential. The style would often be much like a wedding itself with bridesmaids, flowers, hymns, even the renewal of vows made only an hour or two before at a civil ceremony. There were no qualms about blessing the couple.

7.3 Alongside this development was the trend for divorced and remarried people no longer to be denied the sacraments, even for a brief period after their further marriage. This element of the Act of Convocation in 1957 was eventually revoked formally by the General Synod in November 1982. By then it had fallen into almost complete disuse.

7.4 It was only after the failure of 'Option G' in 1984 that the House of Bishops issued a 'service of prayer and dedication following a civil marriage' (see para. 1.10 above). This could only be done following the further revocation by the General Synod in July 1985 of that part of the 1957 Act of Convocation which forbade public services for those who contracted a civil marriage after divorce. The liturgy then published has been commended for use by the House of Bishops, its official authorization by the General Synod being unnecessary as it was not an alternative to part of *The Book of Common Prayer*. The service of prayer and dedication is widely used, and often by clergy who, while they may consider the further marriage of the divorced in church to be right in certain circumstances, do not wish to contravene the Act of Convocation in this matter and so behave in a way which they regard as contrary to the declared mind of the Church.

7.5 We do not propose the abolition of this service, but we believe that, within the national framework we commend, the scope for its use becomes clearer. It is not intended to be used as a substitute for the marriage service. Our overall recommendation would enable any parish priest who judged it right to undertake the further marriage of the divorced to do so with the advice and support of the wider Church and so no longer to act in contravention of ecclesiastical discipline.

7.6 We recognize that there may be some occasions when a marriage in church is deemed inappropriate, yet the parish priest will wish to offer the couple the possibility of beginning their married life after a civil marriage in the context of Christian worship. Here the service of prayer and dedication would be appropriate. There are some couples who are themselves uncertain about the nature and character of further marriage and may not wish to be married in church, yet desire some act of worship with which to mark their new relationship. There may also be some clergy who believe marriage to be indissoluble but nevertheless wish to pray with and for the couple, even if they think that their relationship is not a marriage in the fullest Christian sense. This service may also be particularly appropriate where one of the partners has more than one previous marriage. The complexity of relationships resulting from such a marital history may mean a service of prayer and dedication is the wisest pastoral course.

7.7 It is inappropriate for the service of prayer and dedication following a civil marriage to be conducted as if it were a marriage service in all but name. Such a practice has simply served to confuse. The liturgy authorized by the House of Bishops is deliberately described as a 'service of prayer and dedication' rather than as a 'service of blessing'.

7.8 A further question has arisen as to whether the service of prayer and dedication should be used in conjunction with civil weddings in premises approved under the Marriage Act 1994 (which allowed venues other than Register Offices). However, as this Act expressly provides that *'... no religious service shall be used at a marriage on approved premises'*, the use not only of the marriage service itself but also of the service of prayer and dedication is clearly precluded. This service should not therefore be used where a marriage is being solemnized on premises approved under the Marriage Act 1994.

8: conclusion and consequential recommendations

8.1 Having carefully considered the theological arguments and the pastoral realities outlined above, and while still holding to the Church of England's traditional teaching that marriage should always be undertaken as a lifelong commitment, we take the unanimous view that the Church should provide a common procedure authorizing incumbents, where they see fit, to officiate at the further marriage of divorced people with a former spouse still living.

8.2 In recommending this course, we nevertheless believe that such marriages should only take place in accordance with a nationally agreed set of pastoral criteria, principles and procedures. We believe that it is pastorally desirable and in the interests of all those concerned (including incumbents) that there should be broad consistency of practice on this matter. We encourage clergy to be both pastoral and rigorous in applying these, so as to ensure that there is no presumption that couples have an automatic entitlement to be married in church in such circumstances. In addition, we are concerned to safeguard the incumbent's rights with regard to the use of the parish church and to protect the position of those clergy who conscientiously object to further marriage in church.[1] With these objectives in mind, we recommend a Draft Code of Practice, based on pastoral criteria, which is set out in full in Appendix 1 in a format designed for use by parish clergy (although it can be adapted for use by others as necessary). The pastoral criteria and recommended procedures – the salient points of which are set out below – are based on and largely drawn from the practice in a number of dioceses which have developed considerable experience in their application building upon the 1985 draft guidelines (see Appendix 5).

8.3 We do not intend that the pastoral criteria and the associated procedures should be burdensome either to clergy or to bishops. We recognize, however, that as they will require consistency in application, all clergy and bishops will need to understand them thoroughly so that they may be implemented with care and precision. Thus we recommend that bishops should put in place a programme of induction and training in their dioceses, in order to establish at every level understanding and acceptance of the criteria and of operation of the procedures.

Pastoral criteria
(set out in more detail in Appendix 1, section 3)

8.4 We recommend a careful and considered process by which the couple would be required to satisfy the parish priest in a number of areas before any commitment is given to further marriage in church. Given the difficulties encountered over the years, an especially careful pastoral process should not be considered an obstacle but a careful response to pastoral need. The following areas should be explored:

(a) the couple should clearly understand the purpose and meaning of marriage (i.e. that it should be faithful and lifelong);

(b) they should have come to terms with the breakdown of the previous marriage and should show sufficient readiness to enter wholeheartedly into the new relationship, with evidence of repentance, forgiveness and generosity of spirit regarding the previous relationship;

(c) adequate provision must have been made for any children and for the former spouse;

(d) a reasonable time should have elapsed since the divorce: the further the divorce lies in the past, the less personal and social 'baggage' is likely to be carried into the new relationship;

(e) the new marriage should not be such as to give rise to hostile public comment or scandal;

(f) the relationship between the applicants should not have been a direct cause of the breakdown of the former marriage;

(g) neither of the partners should have been married and divorced more than once;[2]

(h) there should be evidence of receptiveness to the Christian faith (see below).

8.5 In recommending (h) above as one of the issues which should be explored, we are not implying a policy of admitting regular Church members only. Rather, we are recognizing the important principle that the Church cares for couples seeking marriage not as a separate undertaking, as though marriage could be isolated from the rest of life, but as an integral part of the ministry of the gospel. Responsiveness to God's call, whether it be elementary or developed, is the condition for an effective ministry of God's grace in the gift of marriage. If this concept governs the Church's ministry in general with regard to marriage, it is particularly important to have it in view when marriage is undertaken in the context of redemption of the past.

Principles

8.6 These principles undergird the process for handling applications:

(a) the decision whether to conduct a further marriage should rest with the incumbent;

(b) clergy should not be obliged to conduct such services against their consciences.

Procedures

8.7 The following procedures are recommended:

(a) incumbents should discuss general policy on the matter with their PCC, with a view where possible to agreeing a parish policy on such services (recognizing that the last word as to what services take place in the parish church rests with the incumbent);

(b) parishes should have available to enquirers a document setting out the Church of England's policy, and the parish's part in that, together with an application form for completion by the couple;

(c) the incumbent should always interview the couple concerned, applying the pastoral criteria outlined in paragraph 8.4 above;

(d) clergy should, as a matter of good practice, seek the advice of their diocesan bishop (through whatever channels the bishop may consider appropriate);

(e) the incumbent should submit the form and his/her statement of the case to the diocesan bishop (subject to whatever diocesan arrangements may have been set up);

(f) the incumbent, in the light of the bishop's advice, should convey the decision to the couple in person and in writing;

(g) it is at the discretion of the incumbent whether to offer the couple a service of prayer and dedication after a civil marriage in preference to further marriage in church.

9: summary of recommendations

9.1 The following recommendations flow from our acceptance of the principle that the Church of England should recognize that – in the words of the 1981 General Synod Resolution – *'there are circumstances in which a divorced person may be married in church during the lifetime of a former partner'.*[1]

9.2 In order to permit further marriage of divorced persons (with a spouse still living) the 1957 Act of the Canterbury Convocation would need to be revoked in its entirety (para. 4.11). This could be achieved either by an amendment to Canon B 30 (para. 4.11) or by replacing the 1957 Act of Convocation with a new Act of Synod (para. 4.12).

9.3 National pastoral criteria, principles and procedures should be drawn up, incorporating existing best practice in dioceses, outlining the process by which further marriage can take place in church (para. 6.3).

9.4 Incumbents should discuss the parish's general policy on further marriage with their PCCs (para. 6.6).

9.5 Incumbents would be responsible in each case for deciding which further marriages would take place in their parish church after reference to their diocesan bishop, such reference being in line with whatever procedure is adopted within the diocese (para. 6.4).

50

9.6 Diocesan bishops would have an advisory role, ensuring that the correct procedures had been followed and offering pastoral guidance as appropriate: it would be for the bishop to determine how this advisory function was handled within his diocese (para. 6.4).

9.7 Diocesan bishops should put in place a programme of induction and training for clergy in their dioceses in order to establish at every level understanding and acceptance of the criteria, and the operation of the procedures (para. 8.3).

9.8 The service of prayer and dedication should continue to be available (para. 7.5).

9.9 Statistics of further marriages should be kept within each diocese (para. 6.5).

draft code of practice
(for use in every parish)

1.1 Marriage is created by God to be a lifelong relation between a man and woman. The Church expects all couples seeking marriage to intend to live together *'for better for worse ... till death us do part'*. It is not, then, a light matter to solemnize a marriage in which one partner has a previous partner still living. It is important that where this is undertaken it should be on the basis of clear principles that are consistent with the Church's teaching.

1.2 These recommended principles, pastoral criteria and procedures have been issued by the House of Bishops for use by you as the parish priest, as it is your decision as to whether such a couple may be married in church. (They are also intended for use by the bishop and/or his adviser.)

2 Principles
The responsibility of the parish priest

2.1 The responsibility for deciding whether or not to conduct a further marriage rests with you, the parish priest, both for pastoral and legal reasons. You should take the decision within the context of the national guidelines.

2.2 Under the Matrimonial Causes Act 1965 you are not obliged to officiate at such further marriages, nor to make your church available for them. If you are unwilling to officiate at further marriages and your church is not available for such services, you should make this clear to enquiring couples at an early stage.

2.3 You may agree to delegate such a wedding to a colleague but assistant clergy or retired clergy in the area cannot be required to conduct further marriages against their conscience.

3 Pastoral criteria
Issues to be explored and questions to be considered

3.1 You will need to go over the following issues with the couple in the course of your interview with them; suggested questions linked to the recommended criteria are set out below:

(a) The applicants should have a clear understanding of the meaning and purpose of marriage.

- Do the couple understand that divorce is a breach of God's will for marriage?
- Have they a determination for the new marriage to be a lifelong faithful partnership?

(b) The applicants should have a mature view of the circumstances of the breakdown of the previous marriage and be ready to enter wholeheartedly and responsibly into a new relationship.

- Does the divorced person appear to be relatively free of self-deception and self-justification about the past?
- Did the divorced person take the first marriage seriously and has he/she learnt from mistakes?
- If one of the applicants has not been married before, is he/she aware of the possible cause(s) of the breakdown of their future partner's previous marriage?
- Is there an attitude of repentance, forgiveness and

generosity of spirit so that the applicants are free to build a new relationship?

(c) Adequate provision should have been made for any children and the former spouse.

- What arrangements have been made to ensure that the former partner and children of the previous marriage have been adequately provided for in relation to the means of the applicant?

(d) A reasonable time should have elapsed since the divorce was finalized, as the further the divorce lies in the past, the less the personal and social 'baggage' is likely to be carried in relation to a further marriage.

- Has there been sufficient distance of time not only to recover from the pain but also to make progress towards recovery of a new emotional stability?

(e) The effects of the proposed marriage on the church and neighbourhood should be considered.

- Would the new marriage be likely to be a cause of hostile public comment or scandal?

(f) The causes of the breakdown of the previous marriage should be considered carefully.

- Was the relationship between the applicants a direct cause of the breakdown of the former marriage?

(g) Neither of the parties should normally have been married and divorced more than once.

- Has either or both of the parties been married/divorced more than once?

(h) There should be signs of a developing Christian faith and an understanding of the need of God's grace in all relationships (see para. 8.5 above).

- Do the applicants display a readiness to participate in the life of the local church?

4 Recommended procedures

Dialogue between the parish priest and the parish

4.1 It is not only the consciences of the clergy that are at issue but also those of the laity and of the whole community. You should therefore discuss the principles and outworking of this issue with the PCC with a view, where possible, to developing an agreed policy covering services of further marriage.

Relationships with fellow clergy

4.2 It will be helpful if there are occasional discussions at Deanery Chapter meetings on the issues raised, so that clergy are aware of the views of their colleagues, recognize each other's position, and respect the position of those parishes where such marriages are not allowed.

Local Ecumenical Partnerships

4.3 Special consideration will need to be given to consultation with ecumenical partners in parishes where a Local Ecumenical Partnership is in operation.

Documentation

4.4 The documents explaining the national policy should be given to all enquirers, including:

(a) A copy of the Church of England explanatory statement. (To be prepared at a later date.)

(b) The national application form, which is to be completed by the couple, with the assistance of the parish priest where required. (To be prepared at a later date.)

(c) The practical steps which would have to be taken by those requesting such a marriage.

(d) A timescale indicating how long the process may take.

Interviews

4.5 If the couple's request is to be taken further, the background of their case needs to be explored very carefully. When you come to consider the circumstances of the couple, the cause for the breakdown of the previous marriage may not be clear under the provisions of the Family Law Act 1996, so you will have to handle each case with a great deal of sensitivity. This is best done by at least two confidential interviews, using the application form as background material. The first priority of these delicate interviews is to consider the particular circumstances in the light of the pastoral criteria. The couple should understand the purpose of the interviews and it should be made clear to them that attending the interviews cannot imply an agreement to conduct a marriage. Both partners should attend the interviews and they should be made aware in advance of the searching and personal nature of the issues to be discussed.

4.6 The interviews cannot have a standard form but you will need to obtain satisfactory answers to the questions which are set out in section 3 above.

Reference to the bishop
4.7 Although the decision whether to conduct a further marriage rests with you as the parish priest you should refer each case to your diocesan bishop.[1] You should send the bishop the couple's application form with a statement of the case you have drawn up based on the interviews, together with any provisional conclusions that you have reached.

The decision
4.8 After you receive the bishop's advice, it is for you to decide the response to the application. In considering what course to adopt you should always bear in mind the consequences of setting a precedent which it will be hard not to follow.

4.9 You should convey the decision to the couple in person and in writing (sending a copy of your letter to the bishop). Your letter should clearly state the reasons for your decision. Communication through all the stages is very important.

4.10 In cases where the couple's application is refused, and the couple believe that the pastoral criteria and/or the procedures have not been followed correctly, it is open to them to request the bishop to review the case (in consultation with you).

4.11 In cases where you agree to the couple's request, you will need to explain the necessity for marriage preparation (as for any marriage).

5 Services of prayer and dedication

5.1 There may be some cases when a marriage in church is deemed inappropriate, yet you will wish to offer the couple the possibility of beginning their life after a civil marriage in the context of Christian worship. Here a service of prayer and dedication after a civil marriage could be appropriate, although it is not intended to be used as a substitute for the marriage service. However, the reasons for considering a further marriage inappropriate may also apply to this option.

5.2 In 1985 the House of Bishops approved and commended for use services of prayer and dedication after civil marriage. The vows taken in a civil marriage are of course just as binding as those taken in church but the service gives the couple an opportunity to express their commitment before God. The Church witnesses publicly to the permanence of their marriage, while also expressing in a more personal way the love and forgiveness of God.

5.3 If you decide that a service of prayer and dedication is appropriate, and the couple agree, you must prepare the couple for the service with care. You must of course be satisfied before conducting the service that the civil marriage has been contracted.

Conduct of the service

5.4 The service of prayer and dedication should be joyful, attractive and satisfying but it should be clear that it is not a solemnization of marriage. The following points should be observed in addition to the introductory notes found in the service:

(a) While there is no need for a best man or attendants they may be included in the service.

(b) You will want to discuss with the couple the scale of the service such as the numbers present, the choice of music, the presence of the choir and the decoration of the church.

(c) These services must not take place in hotels or other places licensed under the Marriage Act 1994. The right place for any church involvement in the dedication of a marriage is a place of Christian worship.

6 Legal formalities

Divorce documents

6.1 The parish priest conducting a further marriage service must see and check the relevant divorce documents before calling the banns. Particular note should be taken that a decree absolute has been obtained, not merely a decree nisi. The advice of the diocesan registrar should be sought if the parish priest has any doubts about the document(s) presented.

6.2 The Church will recognize a declaration of nullity made by a court in the United Kingdom; that is, a declaration that there is no valid marriage in existence. A cleric has the same obligation to marry a parishioner whose marriage has been annulled as would exist if the parishioner had never gone through a form of marriage.

Common and Special Licences
6.3 These licenses are not at present available in cases of further marriage.

Residence qualifications
6.4 The couple concerned will need to satisfy the statutory requirements regarding residence.

Banns
6.5 (a) It is not necessary (and may be pastorally inappropriate) to include in the calling of banns any reference to the status of the parties (bachelor, spinster, etc.), although this must be included on the marriage certificate.

  (b) If one party resides in another parish or is on the Electoral Roll of another parish, those responsible in that other parish are obliged to read the banns even if that parish priest does not agree that further marriages should take place in church. This is an area which calls for sensitivity towards the position of fellow clergy.

  (c) Where (b) gives rise to difficulties, an alternative is for the couple to apply to the Superintendent Registrar for a certificate in lieu of banns, though one of the parties must have the required seven days' residence in both the registration district and the parish in which the marriage is to take place.

7 Statistics

7.1 In all cases, you should notify the bishop when you proceed with such a marriage service to enable diocesan records to be kept. The information needs to be collected in a standardized format and so you should complete the national form and send it to your bishop each quarter.

7.2 You should also notify the bishop within two weeks of cases that you have refused (as well as via the quarterly returns).

the 1957 Act of the Canterbury Convocation

The following Regulations were passed in the Upper and Lower Houses of Canterbury Convocation in May 1957 and declared an Act of Convocation on 1 October 1957. [The General Synod revoked 2(A) in November 1982, and 2(B) in July 1985.]

Regulations Concerning Marriage and Divorce

1. That this House reaffirms the following four Resolutions of 1938, and in place of Resolution 5 then previously adopted by the Upper House substitutes Resolution 2(A) below, which restates the procedure generally followed since 1938.

    (1) That this House affirms that according to God's will, declared by Our Lord, marriage is in its true principle a personal union, for better or for worse, of one man with one woman, exclusive of all others on either side, and indissoluble save by death.

    (2) That this House also affirms as a consequence that remarriage after divorce during the lifetime of a former partner always involves a departure from the true principle of marriage as declared by Our Lord.

    (3) That in order to maintain the principle of lifelong obligation which is inherent in every legally contracted marriage and is expressed in the plainest terms in the Marriage Service, the Church should not allow the use of that service in the case of anyone who has a former partner still living.

    (4) That while affirming its adherence to Our Lord's principle and standard of marriage as stated in the first and second of the above resolutions, this House recognises

that the actual discipline of particular Christian Communions in this matter has varied widely from time to time and place to place, and holds that the Church of England is competent to enact such a discipline of its own in regard to marriage as may from time to time appear most salutary and efficacious.

[2(A) Recognising that the Church's pastoral care for all people includes those who during the lifetime of a former partner contract a second union, this House approves the following pastoral regulations as being the most salutary in present circumstances:

(a) When two persons have contracted a marriage in civil law during the lifetime of a former partner of either of them, and either or both desire to be baptised or confirmed or to partake of the Holy Communion, the incumbent or other priest having the cure of their souls shall refer the case to the Bishop of the diocese, with such information as he has and such recommendations as he may desire to make.

(b) The Bishop in considering the case shall give due weight to the preservation of the Church's witness of Our Lord's standard of marriage and to the pastoral care of those who have departed from it.

(c) If the Bishop is satisfied that the parties concerned are in good faith and that their receiving of the Sacraments would be for the good of their souls and ought not to be

cause of offence to the Church, he shall signify his
approval thereof both to the priest and to the party or
parties concerned: this approval shall be given in writing
and shall be accepted as authoritative in both the
particular diocese and in all other dioceses of the
province.][1]

[2(B) No public Service shall be held for those who have
contracted a civil marriage after divorce. It is not within the
competence of the Convocations to lay down what private
prayers the curate in the exercise of his pastoral Ministry may
say with the persons concerned, or to issue regulations as to
where or when these prayers shall be said.][2]

2(C) Recognising that pastoral care may well avert the danger if
it comes into play before legal proceedings have started, this
House urges all clergy in their preparation of couples for
marriage, to tell them, both for their own sakes and for that
of their friends, that the good offices of the clergy are always
available.

extract from *Marriage and the Church's Task,*
The Report of the General Synod Marriage Commission (1978)

An explanatory note

We reproduce below an extract from *Marriage and the Church's Task* (1978) to which we refer in paragraph 2.1 of the report. This provides an outline of biblical exegesis supporting the proposals of the earlier General Synod Commission. Some features of this exposition were idiosyncratic, and now look a little dated in the light of further writing since, but the general conclusions are sound and give more detail to the position outlined in our report.

Readers wishing to apprise themselves of further background writing on this subject may wish to refer additionally to the advice which the Revd Professor Charles Cranfield submitted to the United Reformed Church when it was discussing this subject (see *The Bible and Christian Life*, T. & T. Clark, 1985, chapter 17). Professor Cranfield advances an exegesis which is consistent with the earlier Anglican reports, and with the present report.

The testimony of the Bible

102. Thus far we have been reflecting on the nature of marriage in the light of human experience and insight. It might be said that we had been putting forward a natural theology of marriage. We turn now to revelation and its primary witness in the Bible. Here too we have to discriminate between the changing and the unchanging, the substance and its expression. The witness of the New Testament comes to us from a specific cultural context, and we are constrained to keep in mind the distinction between that which is of

permanent and that which is of only transient value and significance.

103. It is fitting that we should ask first, as of primary importance, what Jesus himself taught about marriage. Any considered answer to this question has to take into account both the meagreness and the character of the gospel evidence. On the one hand, the recorded words of Jesus concerning marriage occur, for the most part, in contexts in which he is speaking of divorce rather than of marriage. On the other hand, they show signs of having been expanded and adapted to answer practical questions which had arisen in the life of the early Church, where differing Jewish and Gentile cultural customs obtained. The recorded words afford us access to the mind of Christ, but the mind of Christ cannot be simply and immediately read off the recorded words.

The Words of Jesus

104. The immediately relevant gospel sayings enshrine two basic statements. These are (a) a statement by Jesus about marriage, given in reply to a question concerning the legitimacy of divorce (Mark 10.2-9, cf. Matthew 19.3-8); and (b) a saying of Jesus about divorce, remarriage and adultery (given in varying forms in Mark 10.11-12; Matthew 5.31-32; Matthew 19.9; and Luke 16.18). Further indirect evidence of Jesus' teaching can be gained from Matthew 5.27-28, when he equates the lustful look with the act of adultery; from

Matthew 19.10-12, when he speaks of those who have made themselves eunuchs for the sake of the kingdom of heaven; and Mark 12.18-27, with parallels in Matthew 22.23-33 and Luke 20.27-40, when he affirms that in the resurrection of the dead there is neither marrying nor giving in marriage.

105. For convenience we include some of the material which incorporates the substance of Jesus' two basic statements:

> And Pharisees came up and in order to test him asked, 'Is it lawful for a man to divorce his wife?' He answered them, 'What did Moses command you?' They said, 'Moses allowed a man to write a certificate of divorce, and to put her away.' But Jesus said to them, 'For your hardness of heart he wrote you this commandment. But from the beginning of creation, "God made them male and female." "For this reason a man shall leave his father and mother and be joined to his wife, and the two shall become one flesh." So they are no longer two but one flesh. What therefore God has joined together, let no man put asunder.' (Mark 10.2-9) (RSV)

> 'Whoever divorces his wife and marries another, commits adultery against her; and if she divorces her husband and marries another, she commits adultery.' (Mark 10.11-12) (RSV)

'Whoever divorces his wife, except for unchastity, and marries another, commits adultery.' (Matthew 19.9) (RSV)

'Every one who divorces his wife and marries another commits adultery, and he who marries a woman divorced from her husband commits adultery.' (Luke 16.18) (RSV)

106. In answering the question concerning the legitimacy of divorce Jesus is recorded in both the Markan and the Matthaean versions as asserting the permanence of marriage. He appeals to Genesis to confirm the unity of husband and wife, for here is expressed the will of God; and he forbids men to put asunder what God has joined together. Moses had indeed allowed divorce in certain circumstances, but this was a concession to human weakness.

107. In recording Jesus' saying about divorce, remarriage and adultery – a saying which varies in form from gospel to gospel, probably reflecting the detailed differences of Jewish and Roman divorce practices – Matthew differs significantly from Mark and Luke. They all agree in having Jesus assert that divorce and remarriage involve adultery, but in Matthew's version Jesus makes an exception to 'unchastity'. The precise meaning of the Greek word *porneia* is disputed. The traditional translation is 'adultery', but it may have a broader connotation.

108. According to Jewish law divorce of his wife by a husband was permitted, but there was disagreement concerning the grounds on which such divorce might be permitted. Matthew has Jesus express a strict interpretation of the meaning and extent of the Mosaic concession, whereas Mark has him over-ride the Mosaic concession altogether by appealing to the original will of God. We take the view that Mark is here closer than Matthew to the actual thought of Jesus. It seems likely that Matthew presents us with an adaptation of Jesus' saying in which his original words have been interpreted and applied to certain practical problems of marriage breakdown in a Jewish-Christian community. Further support of this view may be found in the consideration that Jesus' teaching concerning divorce was unlikely to have created the stir that it obviously did (*cf.* Matthew 19.10), had it not appeared to involve a rejection of the Mosaic concession rather than an interpretation of it, an interpretation which, however strict, was nevertheless widely held.

109. We note in passing that a critical scholarly approach to the gospels, such as underlies the judgement expressed in the preceding paragraph, results in an affirmation that Jesus' original saying about divorce, remarriage and adultery allowed for no exceptions. A more traditional approach, on the other hand, which takes Jesus' recorded sayings at their face value, and gives to the Matthaean account an authority and weight equal to that which it gives to the Markan

account, results in the admission that Jesus did not always condemn divorce and remarriage but made an exception in cases of *porneia*.

110. At this stage of our reflections this much is clear: Jesus taught that marriage, according to God's will in creation, was lifelong, and that husband and wife were 'one'. What is not so clear is, first, the precise significance which this teaching has within the total context of Jesus' proclamation of the kingdom of God and his own ministry of challenge, forgiveness and renewal; and, second, how the church is to be faithful to the mind of Christ in developing a doctrine of marriage and a sound pastoral care for all those married people it comes into contact with, not least those whose marriages have broken down.

A New Law?

111. We may hope to shed further light on these difficult and delicate matters if we ask ourselves two related questions concerning Jesus and law. What was Jesus' attitude to the Law of Moses? Did he intend his teaching to be a new Law for his own disciples?

112. These questions do not permit of straightforward and assured answers. The evidence is at best circumstantial and indirect. Nevertheless the following considerations are to the point.

113. There are good grounds for believing that the religious authorities of his time opposed Jesus in the conviction that he was setting his own authority above that of the Law of Moses. Since the Law of Moses was believed to be of divine origin, Jesus would thus be exalting the authority of a man above that of God.

114. Could the authorities have established the truth of their conviction beyond all possible doubt, they would have had unexceptionable grounds for condemning Jesus publicly and unequivocally. On more than one occasion they appear to have attempted to trap Jesus into incriminating himself on this very point; but Jesus did not let himself be trapped in this way. Even over the question concerning divorce, which may well have been intended as just such a trap, Jesus' answer did not give the authorities the evidence that they needed, for his condemnation of divorce was couched in an appeal from the Law, as written in Deuteronomy, to the Law, as written in Genesis.

115. From the fact that the authorities tried to trap him it is clear that Jesus' teaching must have been understood to run counter to the Law of Moses, and in that respect to have legislative implications. It is possible to argue that he was simply abrogating the authority of the Law, but that the religious authorities were never able to secure foolproof and indisputable evidence of this fact. To most of us, however, a reading and assessment of the gospel evidence suggests

otherwise. Jesus was certainly a radical critic of the contemporary interpretation and application of the Law. Instead of its being instruction in the way of life it had been made into an unbearable burden. The demands of legalism had been substituted for the challenge of grace. Jesus refused to discuss detailed issues of right and wrong in these terms; he pointed men back to the source and resource of life and love.

116. So it was with regard to the right and wrong of this and that ground for divorce. Religious debate about the extent of a husband's rights in divorcing his wife misunderstood the whole thrust of the law of life. Marriage was for life – in every sense of that word. Husband and wife were no longer two separate individuals, adjusting their relationship in terms of a nicely calculated less or more. They were interdependent. The life of each was the life of the other. Divorce and remarriage shattered this unity-in-duality as completely as adultery.

117. Jesus rejected all talk of claim and counter-claim. He saw things in a totally different light. His words, therefore, were often paradoxical and disturbing. We may hazard the suggestion that, in replying to a question about the legitimacy of divorce, Jesus cut through the whole tangle of debate about legitimacy with some such sayings as 'He who divorces his wife commits adultery', and that his more prosaic and practically-minded followers tried to turn this

biting aphorism into solid case-law by introducing the idea of remarriage and adapting the saying to the cultural conditions of their various environments.

118. If our interpretation of the main thrust and tenor of Jesus' teaching is correct, it follows that he was not establishing new legislation to supersede the Law of Moses. Nor was he directly concerned with matters of pastoral discipline. Rather, he was calling his hearers to get their basic idea of marriage straight. Marriage is for life. Husband and wife form a new kind of unity. Divorce is as destructive of this unity as adultery.

119. It would be inadequate to speak of Jesus' teaching as setting forth no more than an ideal. It is insight, instruction and admonition. It establishes the character and moral norm of marriage. From this point of view divorce is as unthinkable as adultery. So, too, is the whole idea of marriage breakdown. Nevertheless, the unthinkable can happen. Marriages can and do break down. The Church has to proceed from doctrine to discipline. In Matthew we see, perhaps, how one Christian community took this step. *Porneia*, it was felt, broke the marriage bond beyond repair. In this instance divorce – and presumably in many cases remarriage – was to be permitted. The damage done, this way of repairing a broken situation was consistent with the mind of Christ.

120. From Jesus' other sayings to which we have drawn attention (see para. 104) we can venture the following inferences and suggestions. His equation of the lustful glance with adultery is a similar kind of aphorism to his equation of divorce with adultery. Both sayings are to be taken with the utmost seriousness as expressing insight and challenge. Jesus' sayings about the vocation to celibacy in this life for the sake of God's kingdom and the absence of marriage in the resurrection life may have the same significance. In the fullness of God's purposes all our relationships will be characterised by that depth of love which now we can know only in marriage. Marriage offers in this life the deepest union of one human being with another. But depth is achieved at the price of exclusiveness. Marriage, therefore, is no substitute for life in God's kingdom. The celibate uses his sexuality in this life to bear witness to the universality of love, although his relationships with others lack the totality of body and spirit which belongs to husband and wife. Both the married and the celibate together witness to the richness of the community of love to which God calls men in Jesus Christ.

121. We conclude our discussion of Jesus' teaching by reiterating that there is little doubt about the essential content of Jesus' two sayings on marriage and divorce. Where interpretation of their full significance begins – and with interpretation room for disagreement – we have wished to attribute to them the utmost importance for our

understanding of what marriage is all about. Nevertheless, we have refused to see in them either legislation or direct pastoral instruction, although some of us believe that they must have some legislative import and hence a bearing on matters of pastoral discipline. Nor do these sayings decisively settle the question whether Jesus thought that marriage was indissoluble, although most of us are of the opinion that he cast no doubt on the *reality* of divorce and remarriage according to the Mosaic concession and in fact assumed that man could break the bond which God willed to be permanent.

From Doctrine to Discipline

122. The movement from doctrine to discipline, which we have already seen at work in Matthew (para. 119 above), we can observe again in the writings of Paul, especially in I Corinthians 7, part of which for convenience we quote:

> *The husband should give to his wife her conjugal rights, and likewise the wife to her husband. For the wife does not rule over her own body, but the husband does; likewise the husband does not rule over his own body, but the wife does.* (vv. 3-4) (RSV)

> *To the unmarried and the widows I say that it is well for them to remain single as I do.* (v. 8) (RSV)

To the married I give charge, not I but the Lord, that the wife should not separate from her husband (but if she does, let her remain single or else be reconciled to her husband) – and that the husband should not divorce his wife. To the rest I say, not the Lord, that if any brother has a wife who is an unbeliever, and she consents to live with him, he should not divorce her. If any woman has a husband who is an unbeliever, and he consents to live with her, she should not divorce him. For the unbelieving husband is consecrated through his wife, and the unbelieving wife is consecrated through her husband. Otherwise, your children would be unclean, but as it is they are holy. But if the unbelieving partner desires to separate, let it be so; in such a case the brother or sister is not bound. For God has called us to peace. Wife, how do you know whether you will save your husband? Husband, how do you know whether you will save your wife? (vv. 10-16) (RSV)

123. Paul is here dealing with actual pastoral problems: he is formulating practical rules. He follows the lines laid down by Jesus. His recommendation of celibacy is in accord with Jesus' own practice, as well as with his sayings about the celibate's vocation and the resurrection life. His charge not to divorce is derived explicitly from 'the Lord', thus ascribing to Jesus' utterance the authority of law. No Christian is to divorce his marriage partner. But what is to happen if a believer – perhaps a convert – is married to an unbeliever?

What if, as the passage seems to suggest, the unbeliever proposes to end the marriage if the believer does not abandon his or her Christian faith? Paul has to apply Jesus' teaching to a case which it does not obviously fit. Carefully distinguishing his own judgement from that of 'the Lord', he affirms that the marriage must be allowed to come to an end. It is of less importance than perseverance in the faith. The believer is no longer 'bound'. Whether the believer is free to marry again in these circumstances is disputable, but there is no explicit indication that this is not the case. Tradition has, on the whole, taken it to be the case.

124. In both Matthew and Paul we discern the movement from doctrine to discipline; from principle to practice; from insight and challenge to institution and law. The movement occurs because of the determination to be loyal to the mind of Christ, in both his stringency and his compassion, and at the same time to minister to the needs of men and women in their actual situations.

A Sacramental Union

125. We turn finally to consider a passage in the epistle to the Ephesians:

> *Be subject to one another out of reverence for Christ. Wives, be subject to your husbands, as to the Lord. For the husband is the head of the wife as Christ is the head of the church, his body, and is himself its Saviour. As the church is subject to Christ, so let wives be subject in*

everything to their husbands. Husbands, love your wives, as Christ loved the church and gave himself up for her, that he might sanctify her, having cleansed her by the washing of water with the word, that he might present the church to himself in splendour, without spot or wrinkle or any such thing, that she might be holy and without blemish. Even so husbands should love their wives as their own bodies. He who loves his wife loves himself. For no man ever hates his own flesh, but nourishes and cherishes it, as Christ does the church, because we are members of his body. 'For this reason a man shall leave his father and mother and be joined to his wife, and the two shall become one flesh.' This mystery is a profound one, and I am saying that it refers to Christ and the church; however, let each one of you love his wife as himself, and let the wife see that she respects her husband.

(5.21-33) (RSV)

126. This passage introduced a new dimension into the Christian reflection on marriage and has proved a source of inspiration for many Christian couples through the ages. At its heart is an analogy between the relationship between husband and wife and the relationship between Christ and his Church. Marriage is *'an honourable estate, instituted of God in the time of man's innocency, signifying unto us the mystical union that is betwixt Christ and his Church' (Book of Common Prayer).*

127. In expounding this analogy – for that is what it is – we do
    well to remember that we are dealing only with descriptive
    comparisons, not with exact equivalences or dogmatic
    definitions. Thus, for example, the relation between Christ
    and the Church is here compared with that between head
    and body. However, other images and comparisons are used
    elsewhere in the New Testament. Christ can be described as
    the first-born among many brothers: so the faithful become
    his younger brothers in the family of God the Father. In
    interpreting analogies we must use insight and judgement. It
    would be a mistake to press an analogy uncritically at every
    point. In this instance the important thing is to set side by
    side the unity between husband and wife and the unity
    between Christ and his Church, to allow them to illuminate
    each other and to reflect in this light on the nature of
    married love and the marriage bond.

128. The passage occurs in a part of the epistle in which the
    writer gives advice to Gentile Christians on the manner of
    life appropriate to those who have 'learnt Christ'. For each
    and every status – whether that of a wife, a husband, a
    child, or even of a slave – there is a way of life which
    demonstrates what it means to live 'in the Lord'. Although
    specific demands will vary, this 'way' can be summed up in
    the injunction to 'be subject to one another out of reverence
    for Christ', that is, to be people discerning Christ in and
    through each other. The slave, for example, is to obey his
    master single-mindedly, 'as serving Christ': he is in effect to

be Christ's slave. Masters must give up using threats: both master and man have the same Master in heaven.

129. Similarly, wives and husbands are to express in their mutual relationship a love and care which are a response to Christ's love for each of them. The natural relationship of a wife to her husband is, for the writer, one of subordination, and it is this which gives the analogy its immediate application. In urging wives, however, to be subject to their husbands 'as to the Lord' the writer, while assuming the givenness and propriety of such subordination, nevertheless envisages a transformation in the way in which it is to be expressed. In like manner the husband's exercise of authority over his wife is to be transformed in response to the mysterious working of God's love. Without ceasing to be authoritative it is to be characterised by the self-giving devotion which marks Christ's love for his church.

130. The writer, as we have said, accepted without question the authority of husbands over wives, just as he accepted without question the right of masters to own slaves. Both ideas were part and parcel of the prevailing culture of the day. Christians of other cultures, however, are not bound by their regard for Scripture to accept either. Some indeed would claim, as would most of us, that the historical processes [...], by which ideas of authority and subordination in marriage have been largely superseded by expectations of sharing and equality, reflect the movement

of the Holy Spirit no less than did the abolition of slavery. They can see nothing in nature or in revelation which gives to husbands an unalterable and indisputable right to the obedience of their wives. Any fixed hierarchy of order or separation of roles is to be questioned in the name of human dignity and Christian liberty. It is for each partner to marriage to offer to the other the best of which he or she is capable, and for both together to work out an appropriate pattern for their married life.

131. Disagreement over the issues of authority and subordination in marriage need not, however, prevent us from accepting and appreciating the writer's central point. He is concerned more with the quality of the marriage relationship than with its structure. This quality will be transformed by the reciprocal love and respect which flow from the fact of its being 'in the Lord'. Marriage, as envisaged in this epistle, is a union which issues from love and continues in love, no matter how in any instance it may be patterned and expressed.

132. As a corollary the passage suggests another important insight. Married love – and let us not forget that this includes sexual love – is not to be set over against and contrasted with divine love. Were such a contrast valid, the basis for the whole analogy would be lacking. Marriage is an order of divine love. God's love is creative, self-giving and utterly faithful. Married love can be the same. It is open to

grace. Our sexual and erotic natures may be seen as a providential opportunity given to us by God for learning more and more of the life of love in all its heights and depths. Marriage will be purified and deepened when it is undertaken 'in Christ'. The love of husband and wife for each other will at the same time be a love for God in and through each other and a love for each other in God.

133. To develop the analogy in this way is to develop, in the wider but important sense of the word, a 'sacramental' theology of marriage, which does justice both to the rooting of marriage in nature and society and to its purification and completion in the redemptive love of God. Human love becomes the medium of divine love, in which it also participates. Thus the vocation of those who marry 'in Christ' is to show in their life together, in their unity-in-duality, what love between a man and a woman, within the enabling, forgiving and renewing context of God's creative and redemptive love, can and shall become.

134. To develop the analogy still further, as has sometimes happened, and to affirm on this basis that marriage between the baptised is a sacrament of the Church, instituted by Christ, and that in this sacrament husband and wife are joined together by God in a union which no power on earth can dissolve, is, we believe, mistaken. It is not hard to understand how such a development has occurred. Nevertheless, we are unanimous in our conviction that it

strains the witness of Scripture beyond what it can
reasonably support.

135. It is true that the writer of the epistle, by referring to Christ's
act of sacrificial love on the cross, has introduced by
analogy the idea of a redemptive element into the
understanding of marriage too. Nevertheless, marriage still
belongs properly to the order of creation, and to erect it into
a sacrament of the Church is to risk confounding the order
of creation with the order of redemption and to suggest too
sharp a distinction between 'natural' marriage and
'Christian' marriage. Furthermore, it is to press the analogy
in the text to a use beyond that which it can bear. For the
comparison is not between Christ's once and for all work of
redemption on the cross and the once and for all
commitment of a man and a woman to each other, but
between Christ's continuing love, displayed on the cross and
nourishing the Church, and the continuing love which
husbands are exhorted to show their wives. It is the
relationship between husband and wife rather than the act
of commitment which the analogy illuminates.

136. The fact that the Latin word used in the Vulgate to translate
the Greek word *mysterion* is *sacramentum* provides no
support for the view that marriage is one of the
'sacraments' of the Church. We may quote from the classic
commentary on *Ephesians* by J. Armitage Robinson:

> *The Latin rendering* sacramentum hoc magnum est *well*

represents the Greek: for "sacramentum" combines the ideas of the symbol and its meaning. It is hardly necessary to point out that it does not imply that St. Paul is here speaking of marriage as a sacrament in the later sense.

137. We do not accept the view that marriage between baptised Christians is a sacrament and *as such* indissoluble. Nevertheless the question still remains whether marriage is indissoluble simply because it is marriage. What does the analogy suggest on this point?

138. Granted that there is no explicit assertion that marriages cannot be dissolved, an argument for their indissolubility can be developed from the analogy, if not by way of logical deduction, at least by way of logical congruity. It is inconceivable that Christ should cease to love the Church. Therefore the union between Christ and the Church is indissoluble; and this union extends to weak and sinful men. (Whether it also extends to those who have been baptised, but who afterwards reject Christ, is known, perhaps, only to God himself. The analogy, as we have said before, is not to be pressed beyond reason.) It can therefore be argued that, just as it is inconceivable that the union between Christ and his Church should be dissolved, so it is inconceivable that the union between husband and wife should be dissolved. In this way marriage resembles baptism. Once baptised, always baptised: baptism can never be repeated.

139. We recognise the appeal of this argument for indissolubility. We agree that the analogy affords a strong exhortation that marriages should not be dissolved. As we have already said in another context (para. 100),[1] there is something radically wrong when a marriage does break down. And this is especially true of a marriage 'in Christ'. Nevertheless, most of us reject the doctrine that marriages, especially marriages made 'in Christ', *cannot* ultimately be dissolved and do not consider that it derives cogency from the analogy with the union between Christ and his Church. Irretrievable breakdown *can* disrupt the bond, even more surely and tragically than death. When, therefore, we have said all that ought to be said about the resources for reconciliation and the means of grace which are available to believers, even so we have to recognise the actualities of failure and sin among believers as well as among unbelievers. What we may hope for, call for and even perhaps expect from believers is not always what comes to pass. In the end fidelity in love is of grace, not of law. The resources of divine love are infinite, but they are not irresistible.

140. We do not wish to end this section on a negative note. The deep, 'ontological' union in love between man, wife and God is a treasure which cannot be too highly valued. It is, in its way, a foretaste of God's kingdom. Its fashioning involves sacrifice as well as fulfilment, pain as well as delight. But its attainment is joy, a joy which is to be found not only 'at the

end of the journey', but also in the journeying. We believe that Christians have a 'high' doctrine of marriage which they are called to commend in word and deed to the world.

marriage statistics 1976–96

Marriages, 1976–1996, England and Wales					
	Church of England/ Church in Wales marriages			All marriages (civil and religious)	
Year	1 Marriages involving one or more divorced persons	2 All marriages	% 1&2	3 Marriages involving one or more divorced persons	% 1&3
1976	524	119,569	0.44	99,589	0.53
1977	704	116,749	0.60	104,507	0.67
1978	809	119,970	0.67	114,272	0.71
1979	938	119,420	0.79	115,210	0.81
1980	1,104	123,400	0.89	116,756	0.95
1981	1,286	118,435	1.09	112,894	1.14
1982	1,544	116,978	1.32	111,109	1.39
1983	1,667	116,854	1.43	113,151	1.47
1984	1,985	117,506	1.69	115,312	1.72
1985	3,145	116,378	2.70	115,239	2.73
1986	4,136	117,804	3.51	118,521	3.49
1987	4,867	121,293	4.01	117,095	4.16
1988	5,539	118,423	4.68	120,496	4.60
1989	6,101	118,956	5.13	119,865	5.09
1990	6,597	115,328	5.72	114,865	5.74
1991	6,281	102,840	6.11	107,717	5.83
1992	6,988	101,883	6.86	113,169	6.18
1993	7,164	96,060	7.46	110,795	6.47
1994	7,384	90,703	8.14	110,732	6.67
1995	7,585	83,685	9.06	110,799	6.85
1996	7,270	75,147	9.67	112,841	6.44

Source: The Office for National Statistics

draft guidelines put forward by the House of Bishops in 1985

Marriage in church after divorce

Guidelines issued, in accordance with the Marriage Regulation 19.., by the House of Bishops.

The Regulation provides that guidelines for consideration in each case shall be issued by the House of Bishops. These guidelines are set out in the following paragraphs.

1. In order that the Church may reach a decision on whether the couple are free to marry in church questions will need to be asked about the past marriage(s), now dissolved by divorce; about the present attitude and approach of the couple; and about their convictions for the proposed marriage. None of these areas can be taken in isolation; each will cast light on the others; nor need they be considered necessarily in the order in which they are set out.

2. The purpose of the guidelines is to enable the couple's application to be considered and resolved as part of the Church's pastoral ministry towards them. Whilst the questions raised by each of the guidelines need to be considered in all cases, the detailed circumstances of particular applications may be such that one or another of the guidelines in paragraphs 4 and 5 below may not be relevant, or that it would be right to attach a greater or lesser degree of significance to one or to another.

3. The past marriage

The divorced person may be free to marry in church:

(i) if the relationship now dissolved by divorce was, either in its original intention, or as it developed, one which clearly failed to aspire to the nature and purpose of marriage as taught by Our Lord.

If it is established for instance that the consent of either party to the marriage was not freely and fully given; that the union was not consummated; that one partner had made a unilateral decision not to have children; or that there was persistent infidelity by the former partner, then there may be evidence that the applicant is free to marry in church.

or (ii) where the prime reason for the breakdown of the former marriage was arbitrary action by the other party of that marriage or where the applicant was divorced against his or her will;

or (iii) where a turning to or from Christ by one partner of the former marriage caused an incompatibility of spirit that love could not overcome.

4. Present attitude and approach

The applicants may be free to marry in church:

(i) where the relationship between the applicants was not a direct cause of the breakdown of the former marriage.

If the relationship between the applicants was a direct cause of the breakdown of the previous marriage then the application is not likely to be granted. If the previous partnership had already broken down but had not yet been dissolved by divorce before the present relationship developed, then the applicants may be free.

(ii) where the divorced person demonstrates a mature view of the circumstances of the divorce.

The divorced person, now seeking marriage, needs to be free of self-deception and falsification about the past. If the applicant accepts no responsibility for the breakdown of the previous marriage, then there is probably an immature and unrealistic attitude and the application is not likely to be granted.

(iii) where the divorced person appears now to be free from personal conflict about the past relationship and has faced the requirements for forgiveness of the former partner for actions or attitudes which may have contributed to the breakdown of the marriage.

If an applicant is still bitter or unforgiving towards the previous partner the application is not likely to be granted. If there is evidence of an attitude of forgiveness and of a generosity of spirit he or she may be free.

(iv) where the divorced person acknowledges that divorce is a breach of God's will for marriage and is truly repentant before God.

If an applicant regrets the failure of the former partnership but shows no indication of moving, where appropriate, from regret to penitence before God the application is not likely to be granted. Where the divorced person is aware of a failure before God and shows penitence, then he or she may be free.

(v) where the divorced person is ensuring reasonable provision for dependants from the previous marriage and shows concern for their well-being.

If the former partner and the children of the previous marriage are not cared for and adequately provided for in relation to the means at present available the application is not likely to be granted. If the applicant has taken all reasonable steps to ensure the happiness, security and welfare of the dependants he or she may be free.

5. The proposed marriage in church

The applicants may be free to marry in church:

(i) where the couple show that they are growing in a Christian understanding of marriage in accordance with Our Lord's teaching.

If an applicant shows evidence of a turning to Christ since the former marriage, or shows evidence that through the experience of the breakdown of the former marriage he or she has now reached a surer Christian appreciation of marriage, he or she may be free. If an applicant has had more than one marriage dissolved by divorce, it is probable that he or she has not accepted a Christian understanding of marriage and the application is not likely to be granted. Applicants must be willing to undertake such preparation for marriage as the incumbent believes to be necessary.

(ii) where the applicants accept Christian doctrine and practice in such a way that they sincerely intend to seek God's help in making and sustaining their marriage.

If the applicants show no evident understanding of the gospel and take no discernible part in the life of the Church the application is not likely to be granted.

notes

Preface

1 *Marriage: A Teaching Document from the House of Bishops of the Church of England*, Church House Publishing, 1999.

2 Ibid, p.18.

Chapter 1

1 This Act of Convocation reaffirmed Resolutions passed by both the Canterbury and York Convocations in 1938, but only the former also declared them an Act of Convocation.

Chapter 2

1 See *Marriage and the Church's Task*, paras 102–140, reproduced in Appendix 3.

2 *Life in Christ: Morals, Communion and the Church, An Agreed Statement by the Second Anglican-Roman Catholic International Commission*, para. 61, Church House Publishing/Catholic Truth Society, 1994.

3 'Introduction for the Remarriage of Divorced Persons' from *An Anglican Prayer Book 1989, Church of the Province of South Africa*, pp. 484–6, Collins, 1989, which is quoted subsequently.

4 *Ibid*, p. 485.

5 *Marriage and the Standing Committee's Task*, paras 31–43 (Options A & B), pp. 17–24, CIO Publishing, 1983.

6 *Marriage and the Church's Task*, para. 223, p.81.

Chapter 3

1 J. Haskey, 'The proportion of married couples who divorce: past patterns and current prospects', *Population Trends*, **83**, HMSO, 1996.

2 *Ibid.*

3 C. Roberts, 'The Place of Marriage in a Changing Society', a paper presented to the Lord Chancellor's Conference, 3 April 1996.

4 J. Haskey, *op. cit.*

5 J. Haskey, 'Children who experience divorce in their family', *Population Trends*, **87**, HMSO, 1997.

6 *Marriage and Divorce Statistics, England and Wales 1996,* Series FM2 No. 24, London, The Stationery Office, 1999.

7 J. Haskey, 'The proportion of married couples who divorce'.

8 *Ibid.,* 'Median ages at marriage in 1996'.

9 J. Haskey, 'Trends in marriage and cohabitation: the decline in marriage and the changing patterns of living in partnerships', *Population Trends*, **80**, HMSO, 1995.

Chapter 4
1 F. J. Sheed, *The Nullity of Marriage*, Sheed & Ward, 1931.

Chapter 5
1 See also A. M. Allchin, 'The Sacrament of Marriage in Eastern Christianity', Appendix 4, in *Marriage, Divorce and the Church*, SPCK, 1971.

Chapter 8
1 We have looked at ways in which a couple's application might be considered in cases where an incumbent may refuse on grounds of conscience to solemnize a further marriage regardless of the couple's circumstances. However, possible arrangements such as a parish 'pairing' agreement are not compatible with

current residence requirements (though we note that these could form part of the remit of the review referred to in para. 1.13 above).

2 As explained in paragraph 7.6 above, a service of prayer and dedication may be more appropriate in such circumstances.

Chapter 9
1 See paragraph 1.7 above.

Appendix 1
1 See paragraph 6.4 above. It should be noted that bishops cannot give permission for couples to be married in church and that applicants should not approach the bishop direct.

Appendix 2
1 This section was revoked by the General Synod in November 1982.

2 This section was revoked by the General Synod in July 1985.

Appendix 3
1 Paragraph 100 reads as follows:
100. In short, we are all agreed in affirming that indissolubility is characteristic of marriage as it should and can be. There is something radically wrong when a marriage does break down. Marriages *ought* to be indissoluble! However, most of us reject the doctrine that marriages *cannot* by definition be dissolved. It is only too possible for men and women in particular cases to break the bond which God, in principle and in general, wills to be unbreakable, and to put asunder what God, in his original purpose, has joined together. Therein lies the measure of human failure and sin.

membership of the Working Party

The Right Revd Michael Scott-Joynt (Chairman), Bishop of Winchester

Mr Mark Birchall, General Synod Member and Vice-Chairman of the Evangelical Alliance

The Right Revd Graham James, Bishop-designate of Norwich, formerly Bishop of St Germans

Mrs Sarah James, General Synod Member and Trustee of the Mothers' Union

The Revd Canon Peter Lock (from May 1997), General Synod Member and Vicar of SS Peter & Paul, Bromley

The Revd Canon David Lowman, General Synod Member and Director of Ordinands, Lay Ministry Adviser and NSM Officer for the Diocese of Chelmsford

Mrs Christine McMullen, General Synod Member, Secretary of Broken Rites, and Director of Pastoral Studies on the Northern Ordination Course

The Revd Professor Oliver O'Donovan, Regius Professor of Moral and Pastoral Theology at Oxford University and Canon Residentiary at Christ Church Cathedral Oxford

The Right Revd John Yates, formerly Bishop of Gloucester and Bishop at Lambeth

Staff

Mr Nigel Barnett (Assessor), General Synod Office (until December 1997)

Mr Jonathan Neil-Smith (Assessor), General Synod Office (from January 1997)

Miss Jane Melrose (Secretary), General Synod Office

list of those who submitted evidence

The Methodist Church

The Rt Revd Dr Peter Foster, Bishop of Chester

The Rt Revd Professor Stephen Sykes, formerly Bishop of Ely

The Rt Revd Christopher Mayfield, Bishop of Manchester

The Rt Revd Dr Kenneth Stevenson, Bishop of Portsmouth (on behalf of the Doctrine Commission)

The Rt Revd Dr Michael Nazir-Ali, Bishop of Rochester

The Rt Revd David Stancliffe, Bishop of Salisbury (on behalf of the Liturgical Commission)

Bishops' Regional Groups in the South West, South, and South East

The Revd R. H. W. Arguile

The Revd Dr D. C. Parker

Mr Brian Hanson CBE (Legal Adviser, the General Synod)

Mr John Haskey (The Office for National Statistics)

Mr David Skidmore (The Board for Social Responsibility)

Mr Nicholas Richens (The Faculty Office)

further reading

Putting Asunder, SPCK, 1966.

Marriage, Divorce and the Church, SPCK, 1971.

Marriage and the Church's Task, The Report of the General Synod Marriage Commission, CIO Publishing, 1978.

Marriage and the Standing Committee's Task, CIO Publishing, 1983.

C. Cranfield, *The Bible and Christian Life,* T. & T. Clark, 1985.

An Honourable Estate, Church House Publishing, 1988.

Issues in Human Sexuality, A Statement by the House of Bishops, Church House Publishing, 1991.

Marriage in Church after Divorce, Ecclesiastical Law Association, 1992.

A. Cornes, *Divorce and Remarriage*, Hodder & Stoughton, 1993.

Life In Christ: Morals, Communion and the Church, An Agreed Statement by the Second Anglican-Roman Catholic International Commission, Church House Publishing/Catholic Truth Society, 1994.

Something to Celebrate, The Report of a Working Party for the Board for Social Responsibility, Church House Publishing, 1995.

Preparing for Christian Marriage, Report received by the Methodist Conference, 1996.

The Place of Marriage in a Changing Society, a paper presented by Ceridwen Roberts to the Lord Chancellor's Conference 'Supporting Marriage into the Next Century' on 3 April 1996.